Who's Going to Wash My Underpants?

(Memoirs of a Soldier in the 60's & 70's)

Keith Coleman-Cooke

First Published 2019 © Keith Coleman-Cooke

I would like to dedicate the book to all of the armed forces veterans, serving personnel and the ones who did not come back or are no longer with us and to all of those men and women who are still suffering from various mental or physical health problems.

I would also like to dedicate this book to my gorgeous wife Kathleen who has supported me in everything that I have done or attempted over the past 40 odd years and also to my two sons, Steven and Glenn who have heard the audio version of this book many times and Steven has helped me by putting together the front and rear covers and collating it all to Amazon requirements.

CONTENTS

Introduction

How did it all start

I was 17 I had a variety of jobs from a hotel page boy to scaffolding, from a door to door salesman to a trade mark clerk and from a petrol pump attendant to a factory worker plus a number of others and to be honest I was getting a little bored with life in general and work in particular so it was time to think outside of the box for a new and lasting career.

I knew that the following would be out of the question due to my very limited education and the fact that I had limited practical skills so it was a no to Policeman (the family would never talk to me again) Fireman (to bloody hot) and brain surgeon (ok, I know, I had no brain).

So, what else could I do that was reasonably well paid, it did not matter if you were as thick as shit, gave me the chance to travel the world and fire guns!!! Got it, I could try and join the Army.

Now mother had met and was courting the local manager of a butchers shop (not silly was mother) and he had served in the Army as a Captain in the Royal Army Service Corps and I am also sure that he did not fancy having me living with them if they got married, so he also encouraged me to try.

When most of my relatives heard that I was thinking of joining the Army they just started to laugh, Keith, the skinny one whose ribs looked like a Harp, he won't even get in and if he does he will not pass the basic training.

This book is about my time in the Army and the wonderful 10 years that I had and I only left as I was medically discharged after going blind in one eye, it is about the banter, the humour and all of the other silly things that go on.

I have changed some names and places to adhere to the official secrets act and I have used their initials instead so if they are still alive and read this book they will recognise themselves and can keep that secret if they so wish but all of the incidents are true, although some may be slightly exaggerated and of course I have left out bits that may embarrass others and some incidents that in this day and age may be seen as not very nice and I will try to protect the innocent (ok and the guilty)

There were many funny bits when serving in Northern Ireland and although I will concentrate on the humour I will not go into details of some of the not so funny bits as I am sure that they would bring back some unhappy memories for some people and do remember that many soldiers suffered from PTSD although it did not have that name then and most doctors did not understand what those poor soldiers were going through and they were very often ignored or some other diagnosis given.

Many of the jokes and funny sayings that are in this book were original when I first heard them back in the 60's but many of you will have heard them many times since then and you may think I have just added them but no, they were at one time new jokes !!! Or at least to me they were new.

I will not name regiments that I was attached to or served in but if you were in those regiments or places then you will very soon know where I am talking about and if you are included in this book then I have not named you but used your initials and you will of course know who you are and in the People and Songs section at the end of the book I have given some first names and in some cases where they came from.

Please remember that this book remembers an era when we did not have political correctness and some of the sayings, comments or attitudes may offend and if you are a fan of political correctness or get offended easily, I would stop reading now and pass the book on to a veteran of that era, at least they will enjoy it and I must also warn you that there is a fair bit of bad and offensive language.

My name when I joined the army was Keith Cooke and it was only after getting married that we eventually added my wife's surname to become Keith Coleman-Cooke.

Chapter One

The start of a different life

After thinking about it for a while and having had the piss taken out of me by a brother and another brother who was already in the army, married and stationed in Germany he must have spent some time laughing.

The first thing to do was to go to the recruitment office in Blackheath on a Saturday morning so that I did not have to take time off work especially if they said no.

I got to the recruiting office and spent a couple of minutes looking at all the glossy pictures in the window with a recruiting sergeant smiling and almost rubbing his hands together with glee, his delight improved by 100% when he realised that there was in fact two young men looking at the posters and he could hold back no longer, with a very large smile on his face he opened the door and invited us both in for a friendly chat!!

After a short time we both decided that we wanted to join so the sergeant very kindly helped us make out the very basic application forms, by this time I was gagging for a fag (a cigarette if you are American) and needed to go over the road to the shop, his little face was one of extreme concern as he warned me to be careful how I crossed the road because he had never had 2 men wanting to join on the same morning and did not want to lose one in an accident.

As we were both aged under 21, being the age of consent in those days, we had to take our forms home to get them signed by a parent and go back the following Saturday to take our forms back and to have a medical and complete our entry test which was a bit easy as we only had to tick some multiple choice questions and if you did not know the answer then you could have a guess, we both passed but they gave no indication on how well or how awful we had done, now for the medical.

Both myself and "F" were shown a book full of colours, with numbers on and this apparently could tell if you were colour blind, I went first 68 I said, then "F" went, 23 he said and we both looked at each other in disbelief, we were then told that the other lad was colour blind and for a short while he was devastated until he was told that it made no difference as he could still be a driver.

At the end of the medical I was told that I had failed because they said I had a Murmur on my heart.

I was just pleased that I had a bloody heart but they said that if I still wanted to join then I would have to go to the Milbank Military Hospital to see a specialist and have an x-ray, I agreed and went on the following Wednesday and they told me that it was probably because I was nervous and that I was in the clear to join, wow, at last I had passed something other than a bowel movement, so look out Army, here I come.

Complete with a new flannel, mother's blessing and about £2.10shillings in my pocket I set off on what was to be for me an adventure of a lifetime and there were times when it felt like a lifetime.

In my friend's eyes I had committed a sin, an almost unforgivable sin; I had joined the army voluntarily. I had not been conscripted and was not even running away from an irate father or girlfriend for that matter but then again most of my girlfriends at the time got irate when I did not go away.

After what seemed like an age I arrived at Aldershot. For those of you who do not know, Aldershot on a Saturday night is as much fun as an alligator with tooth ache. I just stood there waiting, for what I don't know but my mother had always told me that if in doubt ask a policeman and there in the entrance hall stood a tall bloke with a pointed head so I went to him, "excuse me", I said "down the road to the end turn left, right at the roundabout, up the hill, turn right, second on the left and straight down to the guard room". I was very impressed, I had not even asked the question and yet he gave me the answer. I can only assume that no-one ever goes to Aldershot apart from joining the army.

On arrival at the guard room I was met by the orderly sergeant, now this chap had one eye and was 6' 6'' across the shoulders and built like a brick shit house and I may add that every time he spoke he had to use a toilet roll and his only qualification for the job was that he had no father.

I thought it was rather funny that the first thing that you are issued with in the army is a knife, fork, spoon and a towel. I suppose that's the assumption that as long as you are fed and clean you will survive long enough to become a soldier.

I was then shown to what the army call a billet which is a cross between a prisoner of war hut and a zoo and most of the occupants look the same.

I must admit I enjoyed meeting people from all walks of life some of the names and nicknames were out of this world. For instance if you came from Yorkshire you was called Yorky, if you came from Lancashire you were called Lancy and if you came from London you were called Smokey, it was only luck that we didn't have anyone from Wallington. There were also names connected with your surname, if your name was Carpenter they called you Chippy and so on. A friend of mine whose name was Winterbottom was affectionately known as cold arse throughout his army career.

That first night we were allowed a short time in the NAAFI but it took a little while to find the place but then we could hear music and followed the sound to the NAAFI and as we entered the juke box was playing "The Eve of Destruction" rather appropriate I thought.

The next day was one where we were to get or uniforms which we were looking forward to, there were 117 men in our intake and the only reason I remember the number was our intake number was also 117, I am not sure if this was a coincidence or if each intake was known by the number of men in it and most of them were 17 or 18 years old and had left poverty for a steady job and a regular wage and most had left the mines to join up.

That first morning we all went over to the cookhouse for our breakfast and we could not believe our eyes.

There was more food than most of us had ever seen let alone eaten, there was Eggs, Bacon, Sausages Beans Tomatoes, Fried Bread, Cereals plus bread and butter (a rare treat at home) for some time we just stood and stared at the food and then we asked if we were allowed to take any, how different it is today!!

Our troop corporal introduced himself as corporal S, spelt B-A-S-T-A-R-D which just let us know where we stood.

After a few days we went on parade to be told that we were to be educated, so when the corporal calls out your name you have to fall in behind the corporal, now as I said, there was 117 of us on parade and slowly but surely most of them had fallen in behind the corporal and there was only about 10 of us left, now this did not surprise me because as I have said I was not very good at school and left without any qualifications or even a school leaving certificate so I just thought that we were the thickest of the bunch and would be cleaning toilets for the morning but as it turned out we had all passed our level 3 Army Certificate of Education on our entry test, wow, now that was a surprise as I had not put any effort into that test and if that made me one of the bright ones then god help the British Army, but because we had nothing else to do we were put on toilet cleaning duties!!!!

Every morning we went on parade to be inspected by either the troop commander, the troop sergeant or the devil himself, the RSM.

Now do bear in mind that as a 17 year old with fair hair I had never shaved but the RSM must have spotted one sole hair and he went ballistic and sent me off to borrow a razor and have a shave like "normal" men and on my return he inspected me again "did you shave" yes sir, "did you take the paper off the razor blade" yes sir, "well young man tomorrow take a pace closer to the razor" yes sir !! He was also the person that you would need to ask if you required to have a shit during the training and he would go red in the face and declare that you had 2 minutes to get back on parade, hence the term "a 2 minute dump is still used by myself to this day, yes I know it is sad!!

It was about this time that I realised that I had signed up for 6 years and if I did not like it then it would cost me £20 to buy myself out of the Army but if you signed up for 9 years it would still only cost you £20 to buy yourself out but you got an extra £1 a week in your wages, so I quickly signed up for 9 years to get the extra money.

Each morning we had an inspection, they inspected your best boots, that had to be highly polished (or bulled up as it was known as) they also inspected your bedding which meant you had to fold your bedding in an exact way and called "Boxing your blankets" and this had to be done in a very specific way.

Now bear in mind that just prior to the inspection we would have to open all of the windows to let out any undesirable smells so when the troop commander or troop sergeant inspected your bed, if there was anything wrong such as poorly boxed blankets or badly bulled boots then you would see the sparkle in their eyes as they got hold of the blanket on the bed and tossed the bloody lot out of the window, for the first couple of weeks it seemed that everyone's bedding was thrown out of the window and when the inspection was over you all rushed downstairs to retrieve your bedding but this was very difficult as it was all mixed up so you could find that when you went to bed that evening you were in fact using someone else's bedding, how pleasant was that !!!

The good thing about basic training was meeting foreign people from as far away as Birmingham, Manchester or even Newcastle and to be honest I could not understand a bloody word they were saying and had never heard of places as far away as Newcastle or Manchester but they also said the same thing about my accent but at least they had heard of London.

At the end of your training period you have what is called a passing out parade and although some people do faint that is not the purpose of the exercise. This is where all the silly little mums and dads come to see their pride and joy prancing round the parade square like a prize pillock.

Afterwards all the staff get together with their parents to tell them what a fine soldier their little boy will turn out to be, even if only that morning they had threatened to stick a pace stick that far up their son's arse that he would be the biggest lollipop in Aldershot.

I had joined in the September and had my 18th Birthday just before we finished basic training and that night we got very drunk, but we were in danger of losing our 48 hour pass at the end of training because we returned to late, made a load of noise which included singing and anyone who has ever heard me sing will tell you that it is not a very nice sound to be woken up by, but luckily for me my step father knew the officer in charge of our troop and because of that he let us all off and allowed us all our passes, which did help to increase my popularity.

At Aldershot we had a squad corporal who was a born artist, no not a piss artist but a con artist and each pay day he would devise a new scheme to remove the pennies from our pockets.

As I remember his best effort was the time he came round the billets on pay day wearing a black arm band and in his hand he was holding a tin with a hole cut out the lid. He then informed us that Cpl Wilson from B Squad had passed away.

Now we all thought this was very sad even though none of us had ever met the man, we all felt even sadder when our squad corporal, Cpl S, told us about Cpl Wilson's wife and five children.

Every man present dived into his pocket and most gave 5 shillings and some of the lads even gave 10 shillings and it wasn't until a few weeks after we left Aldershot that we found out that there was no such person as Corporal Wilson.

With the ordeal of basic training over with we then went on to what the army called trade training. The army camp where this was to be carried out was situated in the West Country at the back of nowhere. The thing that upset most of us was the fact that the 'local' pub was over a mile away and as we could not afford the taxi fare this meant a long walk there and a longer crawl back.

Our first night out we decided that we would go as far as our beloved N.A.A.F.I the place etched in every ex-soldier's mind for ever. The place where pies must be made a fortnight before they can be sold and the beer tastes of weasel piss. The worst part about drinking that beer was that you were up all night running to and from the bog and to be honest it would have been cheaper and just as much fun if you had flushed £1 down the toilet and stayed in all night.

That evening in the N.A.A.F.I the squad that were due to leave the next day were having a final fling, or as some with lesser education would put it a 'piss up'. As we approached we could hear singing, in the cold crisp winters air, we could hear the words very clear long before we reached the building.

There was an Italian with balls like a bloody stallion
And the hairs on his dicky dido hang down to his knees

We found a table and soon joined in the merry making. Now there comes a time when all men hear the call of nature, in other words you want a piss. Now when that time arrives the thing that worries you the most is that by the time you return your beer will have been drunk by one of your 'friends' and to try to stop this each man devised his own method. One of the lads dangled his dick in his beer for a few seconds, 'that will stop you lot' he said and sure enough on his return his beer was still there.

'I knew that would stop you' he said drinking about half of it. 'No-one would be daft enough to drink a beer after a dick had been in it' he said. 'I don't know' I said we all put our dicks in it, yet you drank it. Other men left their false teeth in their beer but of course it never worked. On their return they often found about 4 other sets of false teeth in their glass as well or we had hooked out the teeth and put them in an empty glass so that it looked like someone had still drunk his beer.

The only way to be sure of gong to the bog and keeping your beer was to take it with you and that could look very funny when you went into the toilet and saw a row of men with their bishop in one hand and their beer in the other.

Behind the counter in the N.A.A.F.I we had the 'never forgotten' N.A.A.F.I girl and most of them were young and came from all over the country. Most of them lived there and I am sure that their training included a course on how to handle amorous, drunken soldiers who thinks he is god's gift to women.

One evening we found it a great source of entertainment to watch a young lad of about 18 trying to chat up a 26 year old N.A.A.F.I. girl who had seen it all before. Well, the more she was rejecting him the more he was drinking, it was great fun to watch and cheaper than the pictures. The rebuff had to come and come it did. 'Do you like sex and travel?' she said, 'Not arf' he said. 'Well fuck off' she said and do you know, he did.

It was not all birds, beer and bishop bashing there was of course bullshit and for those of you that are not aware of it the army survives on bullshit. Our time in trade training was no exception, each day we had troop commander's inspection and each week we had C.O.'s inspection.

For the C.O.'s inspection the place had to be cleaner than the local virgin, this also meant that all your kit had to be laid out on your bed, all pressed and measuring 9'' x 9'', the lino floor had to sparkle and be cleaner that the queen's knickers and of course the place had to smell fresh. This meant that every window and door had to be wide open with the bitter cold January wind screaming through the place, it was that cold that I am sure the local butcher used to store his meat in the empty huts and on many occasions I swear that I saw a brass monkey running around looking for a welder.

The great day came and the C.O. would enter the billet followed by all his little plebs, the C.O. himself would be through the place in a couple of minutes and that was the easy part, then came the RSM. Now this bloke was a stinker and rumour had it that he had been thrown out of the SS for being cruel. His main area of concern was dirt and if there was any present then he would find it, under lockers, behind door, and of course his own special little place which was the light shades. Now if we ever did forget to clean anywhere then it was always the bloody light shades and if he found so much as a speck of dust then in his eyes the place was filthy and we would be made to do the whole bloody lot again.

The troop commander and troop sergeant came next and this was the time we all dreaded because they would inspect our kit. In the bed next to me was a little bloke from Yorkshire who I will call Jerry.

Now if anyone shouted too loud at Jerry he was inclined to burst into tears and every week without fail the following would take place.

The troop sergeant would spot something wrong with Jerry's kit and he would then start shouting at Jerry who would at once burst into tears.

The sergeant would then grab the blanket on which all Jerry's kit was laying and throw the bloody lot out of the window. As you know from earlier on this was normal Army practice but by now I was used to it all and I would find the fact that Jerry had burst into tears all too much and burst out laughing, the screaming skull would then immediately leave Jerry alone and come flying to my bed where he would not even look at my kit but just grab the blanket and proceed to throw it out of the window as well. After a few weeks he would not even bother to look at Jerry's kit but just stand there and if I looked like I would laugh he would then walk straight pass Jerry's bed, give his sick little smile and throw my kit out of the window, but unlike Jerry I found it all so funny, oh what fun.

For those of you who have not tasted army food you have not lived and I can say in all truth that I have never tasted anything like it in my life.

When you eat at the cookhouse the orderly officer comes round while you are eating to ask if you have any complaints and a friend of mine said yes. 'There are lumps in the custard sir', he said, 'I've dealt with that' said the orderly officer, 'I've made sure all the cooks have been issued with handkerchiefs'.

Is it not wonderful the way our problems are solved? We all felt that if the cooks tried a little bit harder then they could have made the food absolutely disgusting and rumour had it that the army cooking course was the shortest course in the whole service hence the old army song.

They say that in the army the food is very fine
A pea fell off the table and killed a friend of mine

After tea and after you had done your quota of bullshit for the day the rest of the evening was free and if you wanted to go out you could but as I said before the local public house was over a mile away and in winter that was a long cold walk so the only time most of us used the place was on pay night when we would put on our only clean shirt, a dab of old spice behind the ears, finish off the letter to mum and then off we go. Now in the early days our pay did not run to a lot so we were inclined to buy the cheapest brew which in Somerset as you may know is scrumpy and what a wonderful brew that is. For those of you that are not familiar with it it's a cross between liquid nitrogen and rocket fuel, in other words it blows your head off but it was only 1 shilling a pint. (5p in today's money)

Now this stuff was known to bring grown men to their knees and after only 3 pints you were the protector of the earth but it was very good for cleaning boots, cleaning engines or getting the oil off boats but you must never spill it on your clothes or put it on a polished surface.

One evening after drinking about 3 pints of the stuff three of us were going to kill each other for the love of a woman. Now this young lady was not the prettiest thing that ever walked god's earth and it was only the next day when we saw her that we realised just how ugly she was but also bear in mind how handsome we all were!!! And it was then that we heard a poem that we felt was dedicated to her.

Lottie was the prettiest girl that I had ever seen

One of her eyes were purple and the other two were green

Lottie was a pretty girl or so her mother said

And both her dainty ears were on the same side of her head

Lottie's nose I am more than sure came from an another place

For it started at her forehead and ran all down her face

Lottie's chin was small and square and with that we had some fun

In fact her face was such a state we thought it was her bum.

As you can see from the above poem that love was always on the mind of the soldier and it was helped a bit by the fact that just across the road from our camp was a camp full of women, that's right, the WRAC or to be correct the Women's Royal Army Corp and they were called WRAC pronounced racks and I think that was because every soldier in the camp was trying to get stretched across them. Now some of those girls were no angels and had seen a fair bit of life long before they joined the army and do remember that those ladies could give as good as they got, they did not see our comments as sexist they just saw us as bloody rude and thick.

One of our duties at the camp was to guard, that's a laugh, the women's camp. This was achieved by having one soldier inside their camp and one outside. One evening when I was on guard all hell broke loose from the women's camp. 'Call out the guard' came the shout and we all high tailed it over the road. The sight that greeted us was not a pretty one. Those dear little girls had grabbed the poor young lad who was on guard, taken off his trousers and pants and proceeded to give him an erection. No harm in that you may say, a little bit of harmless fun but before they started they put his penis in a milk bottle.

Now I am sure your imagination will now take over, this poor lad had an erection inside a milk bottle and the more he tries the less successful he is at getting it off.

Nice girls those WRAC, they have class. The sad part of this story is that from that day on the poor lad was known throughout the camp as pints.

Christmas is a nice time wherever you are and the army is no exception, it's a time when you can get away with murder by just saying that it was only a bit of Christmas time high spirits. One morning about 4 days before Christmas I found myself running errands for the RSM and on one errand I had to go to the medical centre and while I was waiting around I saw some things on a table and I asked what that were and was told they are Senna pods and they give you the runs!!

What a fine Christmas present for the RSM. I thought, all heart this boy, so I stole a few, later that day I saw some of my friends and we decided to wait and not give the RSM our present until the next morning which was Christmas piss up day. The next morning I was once again running errand for the RSM when my chance came. 'Tea' bellowed the RSM in a voice that would turn your milk sour, 'won't be a moment sir' said I, all sweetness and light. I then put a little of the Senna pods in the RSM's tea, an extra spoonful of sugar and Bobs your uncle.

A short time after that I was told I could go so I ambled off to join the rest of the lads and the NCO's for the dinner time piss up. The RSM was due to join us a couple of hours later just to show his face and wish the plebs the most insincere Christmas wish that he could muster. Sure enough at about 2pm in came the RSM wearing a very strained look, no pun intended and every few minutes he would leave the room only to return looking older and older. The funny part about it all was the fact that as far as we knew he never again touched a NAAFI meat pie thinking that was the culprit.

I think that every ex-soldier will remember certain items of army clothing and my fondest memories are of the army long johns. They were remarkable things made out of very thick cotton material that made you scratch all day and when worn under combat trousers made you look like you had swollen glands but the best thing about them was the shit slit.

Now you may not believe this but in the bum of the long johns there were three buttons and they were there so you could take your trousers down and have a crap without removing your long johns which was very handy if you were out on the range in the middle of winter and wanted a crap but had no desire to get a frost bitten bum. Needless to say very few men ever wore them and those that did had the rise taken out of them that much that they never wore them again.

While we were in trade training life treated us pretty well. There were women in the camp across the road, beer if you had the pennies for it and of course friends. They came in all shapes, sizes and colours or at least mine did.

There was CJ or to be more formal Cyril John who was of Pakistani heritage but he came from Birmingham. Honest, he spoke with a broad Brummy accent. It was the first time as an adult that I had come into contact with a person who was not white and to meet CJ was all too much for me and

I burst out laughing. CJ took all the ribbing in good spirits and we became firm friends and yes he also took the piss out of my London accent and at times tried to mimic it, with no success at all.

The other member of the terrible trio was a bloke called Johnny, who I may add had the biggest nose I had ever seen. It bent over and nearly touched his chin, I am sure he used it as a bottle opener. He was also pretty small about 4 foot and a fag paper but he had a heart of gold, he had to have something going his way.

The three of us always seemed to be getting into trouble and one Friday was no exception. The curfew for our camp was 10.30pm and as we were big boys we resented this, so being law abiding young men we ignored it but that meant we had to sneak into the camp the back way. That night we were well late and well pissed so it was going to be even harder to get to our little hovel that was called home. Just as we got over the back fence we saw a shadow so remembering the little bit of training that we had we all hit the floor, or did we fall over, and started to do the crocodile crawl.

Now this is hard enough to do when you are sober but when you are pissed it's almost impossible and we were making more noise than a virgin in a brothel as we were attempting to crawl along. With me in the lead I came across two large black stone like objects. I rested my chin on them for a moment and then looked up. Now that's funny I thought, they have legs and looking further up I saw that they had arms with three stripes on the sleeve and a face that could have won the war with one look. He just stood there and did not say a word so CJ being a diplomat said something, 'Fuck off out of the way' was his sole contribution, that's what I liked about CJ he was about as subtle as a charging female elephant on heat, although next morning he let us off with a warning.

The three of us spent that much time dividing our money and our energy between beer and girls that we found it harder and harder to fit in the required amount of bullshit that the army demands.

Our personal kit was in one hell of a state and it was only good luck that we had got away with it for so long. We thought that our luck had run out when one morning just before we were to leave for driver training the RSM decided to call a surprise parade, every man there went white, including CJ. 'Christ we have had it this time' said CJ trembling slightly, 'You have more patter than a centipede in flip flops' said Johnny to me, 'Do something'. 'What can I do' I said 'just look at the state of us', we did and it was disheartening. Our boots had more scratches than Jack the ripper, our trousers had more creases than Barbara Cartland's face and our brasses had that much dirt on them that they looked antique. The morning looked bleak.

There was no more time to ponder in the error of our ways, 'get on parade' shouted the screaming skull. 'Think you bugger think' said Johnny. I thought and all I could think of were the four walls of a cell, I was convinced that this time we would be locked away and the key would be thrown away.

We stood to attention awaiting the arrival of his royal highness the RSM to our squad. We could hear his conversations with the lads of the other squads, 'charge him', 'charge him', 'charge him' said the RSM in quick succession sounding rather like a credit card salesmen and all too soon he was at our squad.

Us three were in the rear rank which gave us a little extra time then in a flash it came to me. Out of the corner of my mouth I said to Johnny, 'faint', 'Piss off' said Johnny full of eloquence.

'Ok then I will' I said and with all the drama that I could muster I then done the most beautiful faint that you have ever seen. 'Get that bloody cretting off my square' said the RSM. Nearly bursting a blood vessel CJ and Johnny, who by this time were clutching at straws, jumped at the chance with both feet, another lad tried to get on the band wagon but after a swift kick in the ankle by Johnny decided not to pursue the matter and both CJ and Johnny helped me off the square like the good friends they were.

But that was not the end of the matter because in the army if you faint and you have had breakfast then that's acceptable but if you haven't had breakfast then they call that self-inflicted wounds and that's a chargeable offence so both CJ and Johnny had to swear blind that I had eaten breakfast.

The town where we were stationed was pretty dead in fact it was that dead that someone suggested that if they held a disco in the local morgue 'it would still be dead' 'but the trouble with that' said Johnny 'is that you don't get any beer, just spirits' 'but there would always be some BODY there' said CJ. Why is it whenever we get the shithouses to clean I am the one that does the cleaning and those two lazy sods do the jokes. 'Come on you two' I said 'let's get this lot done and we can get out'. Now for those of you that have never been in the army let me explain the cleaning procedure. All members of each billet have a 'room job' and those room jobs change each week. This particular week it was our turn for ablutions, army word for shithouse.

Now the only way to clean the bowls properly is to get your hand inside and with the help of a razor blade scrape the muck off. Now this job is not very pleasant and it's not made any easier by comments from the two yobos. 'You really are in the shit now' said CJ grinning that much that he looked like a grand piano. 'You two are that sharp you must shit razor blades' I said. 'Great' said Johnny 'because the rate that you are going we are going to need a lot more yet'.

The next day I had the misfortune to meet for the first time a chap called 'Henry' (not his real name), who, because of the skill of his driving was known as Henry the nut. Now I think that I would have been a damn site safer had I met a kamikaze pilot or maybe even a hit man for the mafia.

There I was minding my own business sat in the cab of an Austin K9 truck reading a training manual, (war comic) when I looked up and saw another truck coming my way. It did not take a degree in mathematics to calculate that it was not going to take long to smash into the front of my wagon. With the speed of a bird and an appropriate oath like 'you silly bastard', I evacuated the truck and yes he did hit it.

Chapter Two

The Real Army

That was the first of many encounters that I was to have with Henry the nut and I often thought he was introduced into my life as a punishment for misdemeanors in a past life and although I did not know it then, Henry was to haunt my life for the next 4 years.

By the time we came to the end of our trade training our circle of friends had grown bigger and bigger and by now there were 6 of us who used to hang around together and if ever we met any women the banter would be that bad that it often scared them away. One night when Tich had fallen in love yet again we decided enough was enough and we would give him the full works. As we walked into the pub Tich was sat with his bird and he was all over it. I tapped him on the shoulder 'would you like a piece of bread to mop that up with' I said, 'piss off' said he with all the charm of a boa constrictor. 'Ok' said Johnny 'let's all sit here and watch Tich on the job', 'he still thinks it's for stirring his tea' said CJ. Now at 17 none of us were great lovers but at that time I am sure that Tich thought an itchy fanny was a Japanese motorbike.

Now the poor girl that Tich had accosted was by now going to a very nice shade of red, 'she has a nice figure' said Johnny '36-24-36' 'and the other leg is about the same' I said 'I heard she got graped the other night' said CJ 'you mean raped' said I, 'no there was a bunch of them' said CJ and we all fell about laughing as she picked up her coat and made a dash for the door and Tich just sat there with his head in his hands.

The last night that we were all together as a group was the night of the squads leaving party? We had all received our postings and mine was to Catterick. Christ, another camp in the middle of no-where, the only good part about it was that both Tich and Andy were also going there. Oh well, let's forget about bloody Catterick for now and get on with the party thought I.

Most of the lads were by this time courting a bird or even two, from across the road at the WRAC camp. Now seeing is believing but I could not believe that state of some of those women. One was that big that I swear she must have been a stevedore in Civvy Street and what made it look even funnier was the fact that her friend was so small that she must have worked as a bouncer for Mothercare. She looked as though she must have shrunk in the wash. I wish I had been able to take a photo because then I could have put it over the fireplace at my brother's house. I am sure it would have kept the kids away from the fire.

Now Tich was that smooth that some said that baby powder would not stick to him even if he was wet and as he approached a rather dishy bird one could see that this boy had a touch of class. 'Anything that I can get you?' he said 'I'll have a large port' she said 'Ok I'll get you a picture of Southampton, now what about a drink' he said. Wow this boy was smooth.

We all watched with bated breath, what wonder boy will say next. 'Excuse me' we waited 'Do you fuck?' 'Well' she said with a smile on her face 'I didn't until I met you, you smooth talking bastard' and away they went together which left a group of us blokes sat around with their mouths open, although I am not sure if it was a set up.

I went to the bar, 'I want a pint, a pie and some words of advice' I said to a NAAFI women who looked like my mother. 'Here's your pint and pie' she said, 'what about the words of advice' I said, 'don't eat the pie it's a week old' she said without batting an eye lid.

The thing about army life is that it is all laughs, we sat there and watched a few of the lads were talking to a troop sergeant, 'that's nice' I thought, the lads being friendly with the sergeant. But it only took me a moment or two to see that while he was being kept talking by one of the lads another lot were putting vodka in his beer.

Now he must have been enjoying it because he was sinking it like a drain and I had the feeling that he would not last the evening. 'He was pissed out of his mind last Friday' said CJ, 'how do you know that' said I, 'because he trod on my fingers as I was walking back to the billet' said CJ. 'He was pissed that's a laugh' said Johnny, 'we found you sound asleep in the bog', 'I was not asleep i was inspecting the inside of my eye lids' said CJ and everyone fell about laughing.

The one thing about this night was that the party was being held in the NAAFI and that was only about 200 yards from our billet so it wouldn't take long to crawl back to our beds and as it was bloody cold that would encourage us to move a bit faster. 'So if we have a bad night we could end up stiff in the morning' said CJ 'and if we have a good night we could end up rather stiff tonight' said Johnny eyeing up one of the WRAC.

The thing about soldiers is that when they get to a party they do not know when to stop. 'I know when I have had enough' said Johnny, 'I fall flat on my face' and that about shows what a soldier's feelings are on the subject, blind worship of the demon drink.

We didn't arrive until about 8pm and even then some of the younger piss heads were falling about all over the place. One dear little soul was having a Technicolor yawn, spewing, by the main door.

Now on the whole I don't mind a chap bringing up his breakfast but the unwritten law says that you should not do it on the pathway. You see it's not very nice for other people to get it on the bottom of their shoes, it only makes the dance floor slippy and some people get ratty about slipping over a piece of lunch time pork pie and if any of the women were wearing sandal type shoes they got a little upset to find pork pie crust between their toes.

For the past few weeks we had all put away a few bob towards the buffet supper and I must admit that it was a work of art. All the sandwiches had little flags made of white paper and a cocktail stick and on the flags were the names of all the fillings, eg ham, cheese etc. There were also pieces of chicken and they also had little white flags on but they were blank. You see the army thinks that by that stage of your career you should know what chicken looks like. 'That bloody chicken surrendered' said CJ 'look it's still holding the white flag'. 'Just get your supper and let's get back to our table' said Johnny as he was sinking his teeth into a lump of chicken. 'What's the chicken like' I said, 'it doesn't like anything it's dead' said Johnny with a straight face and I almost choked on a lump of cheese and pineapple.

The only trouble with having had a good piss-up the night before is that the next day it all catches up with you as you awake you get the feeling that your head has been trampled on by a thousand wild horses and your mouth feels like a pit pony's blanket.

Oh god please help me 'are you ok' said Johnny from behind bloodshot eyes, 'no I'm bloody not' I replied with all the grace and composure of a castrated pig. 'I have a head like Birkenhead' I said 'there is nothing on god's earth like Birkenhead, not even your head' said Johnny as he stood there in his underpants having a good scratch, not a pretty sight. 'Are you ok CJ' I said, there was no answer just a face peering over the top of his blanket. 'Jesus Christ look at that' I said 'CJ you have gone white' said Johnny. Now CJ did not look at all well and his eyes were very bloodshot, 'close your eyes CJ before you bleed to death' I said, 'who hit me' said CJ in a whisper, 'I think he got assaulted by a pint of lager' said Johnny 'I have a mouth like an Arab's jock strap' said Johnny, 'what's your mouth like CJ' I said, 'Like the bottom of a budgies cage' said CJ, 'how did you get on with that bird' I said to CJ 'I'm not that sure' said CJ, 'the last thing I remember was when she asked me to do the dirtiest thing I could think of'. He had gained our attention. 'Well then what did you do' I said, 'I pissed in her hand bag' he said and went off to the wash room.

The men who paraded that morning, in civvies and ready to go on leave, were a sorry looking bunch. There was one or two black eyes and a lot of red ones and most of them walked on their toes, 'just look at the state of you lot' said the RSM, 'if the Russians saw you lot they would invade us by the end of the week, if this is the British army then all I can say is thank god we have a navy' he said, although I bet the lads in the navy were in about the same state as us.

We had a long train journey ahead of us and the only thing that made that bearable was the thought that there was a bar on the train, most of us had to go to London and while some of us lived there most of the lads had to go north.

Now at that time the train journey to London was hours, now that's an awful lot of boozing time and we had every intention of making the most of it although in truth we all felt like death but a little thing like that wasn't going to stop us all getting pissed out of our minds.

The first person to receive our attention was a gentleman with a rolled up umbrella. 'That's the biggest dildo I've ever seen' said Johnny, 'that's not a nice thing to say about the man' said CJ 'not him, the thing he has in his hand' said Johnny, the man was not amused but he did not have the time carry on further because the London train arrived.

We got our own compartment and as soon as the train was on the move so were we, to the bar. You cannot get pissed on the train because it's so expensive you end up broke before you are pissed.

We got a beer but had a pile of beer in our bags in our compartment and started getting pissed all over again. After a while the door of the compartment opened and there stood British Railways answer to Adolf Hitler complete with toothbrush moustache and hat. 'Sieg hail' said Johnny which made us all jump.

'can I help you' said CJ with all the sincerity of a door salesman. 'Tickets' said Adolf not looking very happy, 'now that's a good question' I said 'have you got any' 'I don't need one' he said getting frustrated. 'It's no wonder BR is getting into debt' said Johnny 'every Tom, Dick and Harry getting a free ride', the look of death on his face told us not to push our luck, and we showed him our tickets and he left.

By now we were all that pissed that we decided we would stay the night in London at stalag luft 3 known to most ex-soldiers as the Union Jack club which is situated in Waterloo and very close to the centre of London but at that time it was a bit rough but it then moved to new premises and is now like a hotel for forces personnel and their families.

At last the train arrived in London we decided that we would get a taxi to the club and on our way to the taxi rank we saw a traffic warden. 'Why do they have a yellow band round their hat' asked CJ 'So that people like you don't park on their heads' I said? We got our taxi, 'where to' said the driver, 'Waterloo please mate' I said 'Do you mean the station' said the driver, 'well I'm too f***ing late for the battle' I said, 'funny

funny' he said then drove to the club without being asked. 'Hello boys' said the bloke behind the desk, 'what can I do for you' he said, 'about 5 shilling 10' said CJ and we all started laughing.

After getting settled in our rooms we decided after getting some food inside us we would all go off to Soho. 'Come on you guys let's get something to eat' I said 'no thanks' said CJ 'I can't eat on an empty stomach' 'I can' I said 'my stomach thinks that my throat's been cut' so we all went off in search of food.

We found a nice little steak house and we ate the smallest steak that I have ever seen. After the meal the waiter came up to us 'how did you find your steak sir' he said, 'Well I lifted a chip and there it was' said Johnny but the waiter did not know what we were on about? Oh well that's life.

Leave was over and it was time to report to my first unit and I must admit the very thought of spending the next three years in Catterick camp left me feeling rather cold and when I arrived I felt even worse, although to be fair I did volunteer for Catterick as it was what is called a strategic reserve squadron which means you might get the chance to go abroad which I was excited about but It looked like one of those labour camps in Russia and the bitter cold bloody weather was about the same. I was shown to a long, low brick building which I thought was a garage but it turned out to be the billet where I was to live

As I walked into the billet I noticed that it was a bit warmer than outside but only by a fraction. 'Hello wanker' said Titch who had arrived first so had the best bed space, 'innit bloody cold' said I.

'You are so articulate' said Andy lifting his head from the Beano for a second. 'Is there no fire in this place' I said, 'it's under Andy' said Titch. It was one of those small round fires with a pipe going from it up to the roof. 'I didn't see the fire, I thought it was Andy with an erection' I said and straight away we were back in our old routine.

Life in Catterick turned out to be far better than I thought it would be. On site we had a small friendly NAAFI and just down the road we had a very large NAAFI club which even had a ten pin bowling alley and as I have never played the game before in my life I was looking forward to having a go. We were just sat there watching the bowling when we were approached by two rather dishy looking birds and one of them had what must have been a 42 inch bust. Now being young and naive I thought that she had the bowling balls up her jumper and I thought that I would point this out at the first chance I got. 'Would you two boys like a game' said one, 'balls'? I said, making a casual enquiry, 'be like that then' they said and lost no time in asking some other lads. Just one look at Titch's face and I knew that I had better not say another word. I did the only thing a man could do in the circumstances, I got up and got the next round of drinks in, oh well easy come easy go.

There was also a Christian place called Sandes soldiers home and I cannot remember all of their facilities but there was a canteen and snooker tables and we went there quite a lot and I do not think it was for any prayer meetings.

We weren't at Catterick long when we were told we would be going on exercise, this means a week or two of camping out under the stars, eating nothing but the dreaded 'compo' rations (tinned food) which make me constipated, which is just as well because when you are in the field the only way to go to the loo is to use the 'thunder box'. Let me explain, you dig a large hole, put on top of it a box with a hole in the top, put a screen round it and you have made a toilet. Now if there are a lot of men you dig a long trench and put on top 5 or 6 of those boxes. It's not the best but it at least allows you to have a shit without hanging on to a tree, plus there is the added bonus that there is no chance of you shitting in your own trousers. Now in all walks of life you get the nasty bastards and the army seem to have more than their fair share.

This type of person finds pleasure in putting petrol down the 'thunderbox' and when there are 3 or 4 men sat there they throw a lighted piece of paper down one end. Now you know if you light petrol in a confined space it shoots up in the air. Now because there happens to be a bare bum in the way it doesn't matter and the sight of 4 soldiers running about with no trousers on and blisters on their bum is very sad and I will admit it brought tears to my eyes.

As we were a strategic reserve squadron we always seemed to be going on exercise all over the place but on this occasion we went to Wales and the Brecon Beacons, which is a very large open space in the middle of nowhere and on this occasion it was in terrible wet and windy conditions and near the end of the exercise an office from some other regiment decided he would be prat of the day and threatened me with a charge for dirty boots, for Christ sake, we were in a field and it was pissing down with rain for most of the exercise but I did not hear anything more and the next morning we packed up all the gear and headed back to Catterick but as we were going along the road towards Aberystwyth that bloody officer saw me in my truck and started to wave his hands about now that was ok as I could say that I was concentrating on my driving so did not see him but the bastard then turned his vehicle around and started to chase my truck, by this time I was going around Aberystwyth and saw a large coal yard and I hid in there and Mr Happy the officer drove past and I never heard anything else and can only assume that he did not know which unit I was from, phew, another close shave.

It was not long before I was back at the Brecon Beacons but this time it was with some Yorkshire army cadets from Northallerton and it was a fairly pleasant experience except that one day each section had to cover quite a few miles going to various check points before returning to our camp in the early evening but as it happened the weather started to close in with very thick fog, which does happen a lot in that area but we managed to get all sections back except one and although we sent out a search party the weather was so bad they had no chance of finding them.

At first light I was with yet another search party and as we were going along I told everyone to be quiet and in the distance we could hear them singing and after blowing a whistle to guide them we made contact and they told us that when the weather closed in they found a large hole and built a camp to wait for morning, very sensible and everyone was happy.

There were only two southerners in the unit as most of the lads had volunteered to go to Catterick as they would be nearer home and could then go home for most week-ends if they were not on duty but when you come from London this was neither affordable nor feasible.

A lot of the lads came from Manchester or surrounding places and one day two of us had some deliveries to make near Salford and it so happened that the other drivers sister lived in Salford so we dropped in for a cup of tea, it was like being in a foreign country as I found it very difficult to understand her and she found it just as difficult to understand me, also bear in mind that until I joined the Army I had never heard a northern accent so when she asked if I would like a barm cake, it sounded like bam cake but to my southern ears I thought she said pancake!! I was very surprised when a cheese roll was given to me, oh well.

Not long after the above incident Tich asked me if I would like to go home with him at the week-end, he had asked his mum and dad and they said ok, I was very apprehensive, what if I could not understand them or they could not understand me but when we arrived I was surprised that they were lovely people who did not have a lot themselves but what they had they were willing to share.

Tich took a great deal of pleasure showing off his southern friend to all his mates and their families, his best mate was John G and his father was the same name and they were known as big John and little John and when Tich took me down to their house and introduced me John the elder did not lift his eyes from the racing page of the paper "do they have kettles in London" he said and I thought what a strange question, yes I answered not knowing what was coming next, aye, we have one as well so can you put it on the stove for a cup of tea.

After going to Salford an awful lot and remember Titch lived just off Percy Street where some of the shots for Coronation Street were filmed, I became a fan of that show for a number of years.

When we were in Salford we used to visit the local pub and in those days I would drink a pint of Light and Bitter and when I asked for one most of the pub fell silent, after Titch stopped laughing he explained that they called it a pint of mixed but whenever we went into that pub the barman would ask if I could order the drinks as he just loved my accent.

Back in the 60's life was so very different from London to Salford, the food was also different, in London we had never heard of curry sauce with chips and when I was first asked I almost threw up but when persuaded to try it I loved it but when I asked for curry sauce back in London I was viewed with suspicion or almost pity.

Titch's mum asked what we fancied for dinner on a Saturday and I said that in London we often had chipolata's, this brought a roar of laughter from all of the family as they had never heard of that term but later that day Titch and I helped his mum with the shopping and as we passed the butchers I saw rows of chipolata's, I was very excited, look, you do sell them here and again amid laughter I was informed that they were called "Thin Links"

The coach to Salford from Catterick left at about 17.30 on a Friday night and cost £1-1/- now bear in mind we were earning about £5-10/- that was pretty expensive and of course also bear in mind that a pint of mixed in Salford was 10d about 5p now!!!

Titch and I decided to buy a car between us and we got a Mk 1 Consul which enabled us to take 3 of the lads to Manchester on a Friday night for 10/- each this not only paid for our petrol but it also paid for a few pints.

One of my fond memories is that as soon as we arrived in Salford on a Friday evening we would have something to eat and the go to the pub.

They would have a band playing and any one could get up and sing if they wanted to and the band would try to encourage as many people as possible to have a go and this was long before we started calling it karaoke and young John G would always get up and sing the same song every time and that was "In Dreams" by Roy Orbson and I must admit he sang it magnificently and that was without any words being projected onto a screen.

Other friends at that time included a very strong accented Yorkshire man who we called cannonball after the very good TV series about a truck driver and he was the one who derided all people that had Yorkshire pudding with their roast dinner as in Halifax where he came from they always had the Yorkshire pudding first, on a plate, on its own with just onion gravy and at that time I had never heard of that, those northern lads were a scream and I was being educated on a daily basis and learning all about their northern charm plus of course there were lads from all over the UK and places that I had never heard of in those days such as Cardiff, Glasgow, Aberdeen and I even had a friend from a place called Thurso in the far north of Scotland but very few southerners and that remained the same throughout my army career, lots from Scotland and the north of England.

Life in the Army in those days was hard but good fun and yes there were times when you wanted to get out of the Army and I had a Scottish mate called Jock (that was a surprise!!) who told me on a number of occasions that he wanted to get out of the Army and I thought that he was going to save up and buy himself out.

One day I had been out working and on my return I went to the billet and saw that Jock's bedding was not there and his locker was empty but nobody was sure what had happened or where he was, I asked at the guard room and all they would tell me is that he was admitted to the hospital, wow, I did not even know he was not well so I immediately went to the hospital to visit, to be told he could have no visitors but as luck would have it I knew one of the nurses and she let me go to his individual room, wow, he must be seriously ill, private room, no visitors and when I went into his room I was shocked to see him sat in a chair reading a book.

What on earth is going on I asked and he told me that he went to see the padre and told him that he was getting suicidal because every time he went into the shower and saw men either naked or in their underpants he would get an erection and felt the need to masturbate.

The padre felt that he had to report this and Jock was immediately taken out of the camp to the hospital and it was only a matter of days before he was discharged as a homosexual, the word gay had not been used in this context at that time and of course, now days it does not matter if you are gay but Jock was very clever and found a way out of the Army that cost him nothing.

Over the years I met a number of soldiers who were friends of mine who admitted to me and our small circle of friends that they were gay but we kept quiet as they wanted to stay in the Army, how things have changed and as far as those gay soldiers are concerned I am sure that would say, things have changed for the better.

Titch's mate John G was also in the Army and he was stationed just outside of Blackpool and we arranged with him to go there for the week-end and as we were serving soldiers they gave us a bed for a couple of nights.

I had never been to Blackpool and to see the lights was fantastic, I was driving and looking around when Titch and John both started getting excited and saying look, that is the famous Blackpool Tower but as I was looking at the Tower I felt the road getting bumpy and then realised that the road had turned but I had not and I was on the tram lines, luckily there were no trams coming and I had not gone far so it was pretty easy to turn round and get back on the road. Phew.

On another occasion a car load of us went to Whitby on the coast and I got the short straw and had to drive but as we were parked up along the seafront I could see a copper approaching, now as we had no road tax on the car this could have been a problem but as we were having some chips at the time I half sat on the bonnet with my chip paper open wide and the copper stopped had a chat, told us he was an ex-serviceman and he then went on his way without noticing that we had no road tax.

Of course, he may have noticed but let it go as we were soldiers and that gave the rest of them the excuse to get pissed and we spent most of the journey back to Catterick singing "Monday Monday"

We also had many married friends who lived in local married quarters but as it was over 50 years ago I am afraid that I have forgotten their names but one in particular I used to baby sit for him and his wife, they had a little boy about 18 months old and on one occasion he woke up and was pointing at his nappy.

Now luckily my sense of smell was pretty good when I was younger and was sure that I could not smell shit so it was just very wet but also remember we did not have the modern disposable nappies but the old Terry nappies and I had never changed one so before I took his nappy off I had to remember where the safety pins went and of course I had to search around for a clean one but if I do say so myself, I made a pretty good job of it and my mates wife was very impressed.

Another time when we ventured further north was when one of the lads, I think it was Rags, was getting married to a girl from Newcastle, I think she may have been a nurse in the hospital and a few of us were invited but I made it clear that as it was a wedding and there would be booze available I was not going to drive but then our Geordie mate said that his mum and dad were going away that week-end and we were welcome to stay there for the night.

All I remember is that it was a block of flats near to the Proctor and Gambol factory and the wedding was lovely but as we were all waiting to go to the reception one of her uncles informed me that it would be a great reception as they had a large barrel of scotch wow.

Bloody hell, now although I do not generally drink whisky I was willing to make an exception on this occasion, just to help them out but as a southerner how the bloody hell was I to know that the barrel of scotch was in fact called "scotch bitter" it was not whisky but beer!!!

A few days after the wedding I got a small parcel in the post with the postmark Newcastle and in the parcel was a pair of my underpants which I had left under the pillow on his mum's side of the bed, she did put in a little note saying that she had washed them for me, how bloody sweet, I did not live that down for some time.

Tich and I had another friend who kept going on about leaving the army and he was a lot older than us and he was very religious but he did not go the local army church but went to what was known in those days as a happy clappy church in the town of Richmond (Yorkshire not Surrey) and he had been trying to get Tich and I to go with him so one day we said yes we would go and it was a bit of a surprise as most of the congregation were singing on their own and praising the lord.

Then all of a sudden this man in a wheelchair jumped up out of the wheelchair shouting "praise the lord I have been cured and can now walk again" now I may be wrong but I was sure that this was the same man that I had seen in town a couple of weeks previous pushing a lady in a wheel chair, the power of belief is amazing.

Another part of army life is that every so often all soldiers have to go on the rifle ranges. Now it must be more fun to put your hand in a hippo's mouth than to go to the ranges in bad weather and after a while it even gets boring.

This day we had been there about 4 hours when we all had to shoot yet again. About 20 of us laying their rifles at the ready waiting for a target to appear when from the left hand side of the range walked an old sheep. It had just about got on to the range when the order came to fire. Now every one of us forgot about the target and aimed our rifles at the old sheep. Now each soldier had 25 rounds and this old sheep walked right across the range, at three hundred yards and about 500 rounds of ammo between us, you may well have laughed to have seen a sheep walk away without a scratch.

We had only been in Catterick a few weeks when we heard that a new draft were coming in from Somerset, great, there may be a few blokes that we knew. 'This place needs more young blood' said Tich 'only because yours is too hot' I said.

When Tich knows something that you don't know he gets this very irritating sneer on his face, 'your best mate is coming here' said Tich. I did not like the sneer on his face so I decided not to rise to the bait, 'who's that then' I said, trying to sound as though I could not care a monkey's toss who it was. 'Henry the nut' said Tich waiting for my reaction. He got it ' Who the fucking hell sent that little bastard here' I said' 'what have I done to deserve this' I said looking up to heaven as though I was expecting an instant answer, all I got was instant laughter.

A couple of weeks later 5 new men arrived, well to be honest there was 4 men plus Henry, who was all smiles with his large, yellow, crooked teeth and kitbag full of shrunken heads. 'Hello Henry' I said trying to be friendly, 'killed anyone lately', 'I am glad I have been posted here with you lads, you are so much fun' said Henry, I wish I could say the same about Henry but to be honest I would find a hospital for lepers more fun than him.

It was not long before Henry was up to his old tricks, he must do it on purpose because no-one can be born that stupid.

One morning just after Henry's arrival I was folding up a camouflage net on top of a truck when bullock brains jumped in and roared away with me hanging on for grim death on the roof of the truck.

It was pure luck that he had to stop at the gate or I may have been hanging on there the rest of the morning. Of course I reported him to the troop sergeant but when I told him I swear that I saw a wet patch on his trousers and as he could not speak for laughing I decided not to pursue the matter.

A couple of months later we went on a large exercise and 22 army trucks left Catterick to drive all the way to Hampshire and what a journey it turned out to be. When we set out from Catterick the weather was terrible with heavy snow and freezing black ice and we had not gone far before one of the lads had an accident. We carried on and the convoy was soon split up so everyone made their own way towards Hampshire.

I was part of a small group who had stayed together, there was Tich, Henry and myself. It was not long before Henry was doing his stuff. We came to a roundabout and Henry put on his brakes too hard and started to slide, he lost control of the truck and it was no surprise that he slid into a bus that was on the roundabout. He said later that because he could not stop on the roundabout he planned to go round again and stop behind the bus but as he came up behind the bus, which by this time had stopped at the side of the road, he put on his brakes and slid straight into the back of the bus. It was lucky for Henry that I was still there otherwise I am sure the bus driver would have killed him.

After driving through Leicester I had lost the other two so I made my own way to Hampshire and when I arrived there were only three other trucks there. Now as I was the 21st truck to leave Catterick you can imagine my surprise. We had not been there long when the phone started to have a fit and for that matter so did the troop commander. Every time the phone rang it was one of the lads reporting that they had an accident and surprise surprise one of them was Henry. Now when the tow truck went out to get him he was not at the location where he said he was. They went up and down this stretch of road a couple of times and at last saw Henry at the side of the road. 'Where is your truck' asked the tow crew, 'over there' said Henry pointing behind a large hedge. He said he had gone through the hedge, through a flint wall, hit two apple trees and somehow still managed to hit a cottage. When I asked him what happened this is what he said. 'I was driving along the road when all of a sudden I saw a lady with a pram coming up my side of the road, what could I do? Well I panicked and I closed my eyes and put on the brakes. There was a lot of smashing and bashing and when I opened my eyes I thought that I was in heaven but I was only in this man's front garden, that's a true story.

In the spring and summer the army went on many exercises, sometimes on our own and sometimes with other regiments and on one particular exercise we were working with the Navy and went to Portsmouth where we spent a few day on a Navy aircraft carrier which for us was a great experience for a few reasons.

First, we spent some time below deck maneuvering the vehicles about and as a young person I did not realise how much room there is below decks on an aircraft carrier then of course there was the food which compared to Catterick was out of this world and finally and probably the most important thing was that in those day the Navy got a daily rum ration.

A lot of the lads did not like nor drink rum so they would swop their ration for other things like cigarettes and although the ration was very generous if you watered it in half it was still very strong so as you can imagine there was loads of rum being offered to us at very cheap prices which we thought was great.

Early summer was now with us and about this time we went on yet another exercise, this time to Morecombe, only this one was different in that it only lasted a couple of days, we all went into town to have a drink and a good time when a copper came into the pub and asked if we were soldiers from the camp and told us that we had to go back to the camp immediately and when we got there we were told that we were all being recalled to Catterick. 'I wonder what's up' I said to Tich 'well it's not me for sure' said Tich. I don't think he has got over his last love affair yet. We were then all told that we were to go on leave for a few days and then we were going on a United Nations tour of Cyprus for 9 months, although that summer in England was not bad it was not a patch on Cyprus.

Chapter Three

Off to Cyprus

We only had a long week-end to pack before going so rather than spend loads of time and money going back home I phoned mother, told her what was happening and then we spent the week-end in Salford, when we drove there we had the thought that maybe it would be better to leave the car in Salford rather than in an empty barracks in Catterick but when we started to tell Titch's friends and family somebody offered us £30 for the car which was £15 each or the equivalent or 3 weeks wages, now that was a result as we had the money to fund a really great week-end, and as the world cup was on we did not know if we would be able to see it in Cyprus and also remember that we did not know then who was in the final. This was in June 1966 and we had a Captain in our squadron who came to Cyprus with us and although I did not realise it at the time but he was also the C.O. of a regiment that was going to Northern Ireland about 7 years later.

They were short of men so our squadron supplied men, one of which was me and about 35 years later we lived very near to each other and he encouraged me to take up politics and become a local councillor.

The great day came and it was to be the first time that I had ever flown in a plane. All the old soldiers were trying very hard to put the wind up those of us who had never flown before. The plane was an old turbo prop type and we were not even in the air when the black humour started. 'I hear the pilot was pissed last night' said one of the lads, 'I saw him trying to find the front of the plane but he could not see the thing through his dark glasses' said another and as soon as we had taken off the humour carried on. 'Look the wings are falling off' said Fred, I looked and sure enough the wings were moving. Now I am not the sort that likes to make a fuss but if the wings are falling off then feel that it's my duty to inform someone but I must admit that I felt rather silly when I was told that they are supposed to move because if they didn't then they would fall off. The lads, or should I say louts, found all this very humorous and I vowed to myself that in future I would take no notice of their childish and immature games, the rest of the flight was very good except for a minor incident when the hostess slipped and deposited three half empty breakfast trays on my lap. The worst part was when it took me 10 minutes to realise that the thing between my legs was in fact one of the sausages left there by the hostess. Days later I was still finding bits of mushroom in my pockets and I did not think the coffee stains would ever come out.

Cyprus was a smashing country for goats, donkeys etc but we found it rather restricting. We had to wear UN uniform at all times outside the camp which of course does not endear you to the local population who did not want us there in the first place.

Although we had to wear uniform when we went out, we got out and about quite a lot. After our first week in Cyprus we were allowed to go to the beach in Famagusta on the Sunday if we were not on duty, we started to get undressed to put our swimming trunks on when we all realised that the sand was so hot it was burning our feet, we had never known this in England.

I put down a towel and carried on getting into my trunks when I became aware that a small boy was just stood staring at me, check trunks, everything is ok so I said hello do you speak English, yes he said, are you ill? No I am not but why do you ask? Because you are so white I thought that you were very ill, aarh, bless him.

Later that night I started to feel ill and started to be sick and shaking, so the next morning they admitted me to hospital with severe sunstroke and I was in hospital for a week.

I was admitted to the Austrian field hospital where most UN soldiers would go, so there were soldiers from many different countries but there was an Irish lad there who was the only other patient to speak English.

He was funny and one of his hobbies was to collect stamps with matching dates, his father had started on the 4-4-44 and the 5-

5-55, this soldier was delighted to tell me that he now had 6-6-66, I could hardly contain my bloody excitement.

When the consultant who was the CO came round he told us that the world cup final was on the TV that evening and would we like to watch it and as I was almost better I thought that was great and he told us that he would ensure that we had saved seats and the staff would come and get us just prior to kick off, when we went outside there were hundreds of chairs but right at the front there were 3 big wing backed armchairs, the CO had the middle one with paddy and myself sat in the other two, now bear in mind that this was the Austrian field hospital and all of the staff and most of the patients supported Germany, wow what a result, the only down side was that we were in hospital and therefore could not get a drink to celebrate.

Another of our outings was to go to the beach in Kyrenia on a Sunday if we were not on duty, this beach had a bar on the beach and you could also get a very good meal there, I think the locals called it 3 mile beach as it was a very long wide sandy beach.

The first time we went there we took a football and as there were about 12 of us we decided to play 6 a side but as we started loads of local kids came out so we started to take them onto one side or the other.

When our 6 a side match had escalated to 20 a side we thought that next week we would bring more footballs and have a number of 6 a side games, what we did not foresee was that most of the local kids turned up and we ended up having loads of 6 or even 8 a side games with us lot refereeing, not what we had in mind but great fun.

We only stopped going there when the owner of the beach bar and restaurant started to give me rather large portions of food and beer so that I would chat up his daughter, who I might add, was rather a large portion herself. I left the place that fast that I am sure I created a sand storm.

We used to start work about 07.30 but we were finished by 1300 so that gave us plenty of time to have a dinner time piss up. What was rather handy was the fact that the camp had its own sauna so we would fall out of the club three sheets to the wind, (pissed) and fall into the sauna and after an hour or so you walked out stone cold sober which meant that you were more than ready for a sleep, tea and then the evening session.

After about 3 months with only part of Sunday's off to go to the beach, the British Army would treat you to 4 days R & R (rest and recuperation, or romp and resuscitation) and that would mean 4 days at RAF Akrotiri and by a huge coincidence the Limassol wine festival was also on at that time, you paid 1/- to get in and 1/- for an empty carafe and 1/- for a glass so for a total of 3/- you could get totally shitfaced on local Cypriot wines, which I might add, are very good.

You would take your glass to one of the many stalls, they would put a small amount in the glass for you to taste and if you liked it then they would fill up your carafe, if you did not like it you then moved on to another stall and when you found one you liked you could either keep going back to that stall to fill up your carafe or just keep trying as many as possible.

Now as you can imagine we were only young soldiers and had never known this very cheap wine back in the UK and most of us had either never drunk wine before or if we had it was just the odd glass.

I think there was 4 or 5 of us and we were all getting rather shitfaced and I cannot remember the exact details (no, I honestly can't) but 3 or 4 of us ended up in the local police station and we all thought that this would get us into massive trouble, then we heard a familiar, but rather poshed up voice at the front desk, we were then taken to the front desk and lo and behold it was Geordie Fred who told the police that he was our troop officer and that he would ensure that we got back to camp and to our utter surprise they agreed to let us go and to be honest I think they were just glad to get rid of us.

In our squadron club, where the booze was very cheap, they sold Tennent's Lager and on each can there was a picture of Ann

Margaret, a well-known actress at that time, in different poses.

I think there must have been about 12 poses in the series but some were harder to find than others but I managed to get the full set which did impress the C.O. on one of his inspections as I had them lined up on the top of my locker.

One of the other camp entertainments was the pictures. It was an open air picture house with hard wooden seats so that you could tell the ones going to the pictures as they had pillows under their arms.

The worst thing about the pictures was that they were next to a helicopter landing pad and every time a helicopter landed the screen would sway about, very off putting and when that happened the lads would throw beer cans at the screen, which was ok but for ages after you had beer running down the screen and that could be more off putting than the helicopters. It was handy if you were skint because you could sneak in after the lights went out by crawling under the fence which was only made of hessian but you had to make sure that you didn't knock over the beer or there would be an outcry and you would get caught.

Bearing in mind that I had left school at 15 with no qualifications, no school leaving certificate and the headmaster telling me how thick I was and he was probably right, but in Cyprus both Titch and myself used to write home every Sunday and the first time we did it, he had finished a couple of pages and I was still only halfway down the first page.

"why are you taking so long" he said and when he looked over my shoulder he realised that I was writing in block capitals, he asked me if I knew how to do joined up writing and when I admitted that I had never been taught he said that he would help and in a few months Titch had achieved what 10 years of schooling could not achieve and from then on I was writing the same as most other lads.

Taking everything into account life in Cyprus was not so bad. The worst part being almost total lack of women and if you wanted a woman the only place to find one was at the local whorehouse. We had been talking about this in the presence of Henry and to see his little face light up made it obvious that this young man had not lost his cherry, (virginity) yet. Well, being public spirited young men we decided to help. 'Change your underpants Henry' said cold arse, (Winterbottom), 'we are going to make your eyes sparkle'. Titch joined us and the four of us headed for down town Nicosia by taxi. The local whore house was split up into eight cubicles but they were only made of hardboard so it was very easy to hear what was going on in all the other cubicles. When I left Henry his eyes were alight with anticipation and I could have sworn that he was about to wet himself with excitement. We had only been there a few minutes when all hell broke loose.

I could hear this girl shouting and screaming and I could also hear Henry making lame excuses. After we had all finished we met in the hallway.

Henry was sat there looking rather rejected. 'What happened' I said, 'it sounds like you had the clap' said Titch. 'Well she was not very good' said Henry. The girl then came into the hallway waving her arms and shouting, cold arse started to laugh, 'she reckons you are a poof Henry' said cold arse, by now unable to stifle his laughter. 'You had a limp bishop' said Titch, 'but I still had to pay her or she was going to keep my clothes' said Henry and I am sure our laughter could have been heard the other side of Nicosia.

The next special event on our calendar was my birthday and we decided for obvious reasons not to go out but to have a piss up on camp instead, that way it did not matter how pissed we got because there was always someone that would see you to your pit (bed) The great day dawned and it was my birthday, I was working in the morning but as soon as I finished I headed to the club where I was about to give my liver something to complain about. When it's your birthday in the army the lads are great, they pile booze down your throat until it comes out of your ears and that lunchtime was no exception and by the end of the session I was well and truly pissed. 'It's a sauna job' said one of the lads, 'we must get him sober so that we can get him pissed again tonight' said cold arse, who was always the logical one. Sure enough by 6 we were all sober enough to go to the club and by five past six we all had a beer in our hands.

By 11pm when the club closed we were all well gone so we decided to take some booze back to cold arse's billet and have a party.
It was a pity that the lads already asleep were not keen on the party but a free bottle of brandy can get anyone in the mood. We had been drinking for another couple of hours when we started to talk, no, mumble; about flying so I stood on the windowsill by way of demonstration. I was that full of brandy that I did not stay on the windowsill very long, that's because I fell out of the window and some prat, (I still suspect cold arse), had put up a clothes line. Now I don't know about flying but I am sure the buggers were trying to hang me. I had the mark around my neck for ages afterwards. On trying to get back into the party I fell into a

large irrigation ditch that was full of water, Christ they are trying to drown me now I thought. 'Sod you all, I'll swim home' I said in a gurgling sort of voice and it was at that point that they dragged me out. 'Take him back into the party, he'll be safer there' said one of the lads but it was only a matter of time before I got into more trouble and that came in the form of one of those rather large coke signs that cold arse had hanging on his wall by a 4 inch nail. To start with it fell off the wall and as none of us were capable of putting it back we decided to leave it laying on the table until morning. We were rather silly and pissed because we left it with the nail pointing upwards and a short while later I flaked out over the table and it was only luck that I put my arm across my face because the nail went right into my arm, which I might add, woke me up pretty fast and as I jumped up the sign came with it.

Now this left me with a large hole in my arm and as there was a lot of blood the lads decided to put me in bed. I think the real reason for this was that if I was going to bleed to death then I may as well make a mess in my own billet but in the morning it still looked very bad and they sent me to the medical centre to get it looked at.

After the return from the medical centre, where they encased my arm in plaster from the wrist to the shoulder, I was put on light duties which meant that I did a bit of one armed office work for about a week. Saluting was also great fun with your arm in plaster.

It was about this time that we were having a lot of trouble with the entrance to our compound due to the fact that the gate was very narrow and only just wide enough for a ten tonner to get in, which resulted in a lot of people giving the gate a clout every time they came in. One day while I was working in the office the troop commander and troop sergeant called me outside. 'Do you think that gate is too narrow' said the troop commander to me. 'Yes sir, it could do with being a couple of feet wider' I said BANG!!! Low and behold it was wider. What happened was that while we had been talking Henry had come into the compound a little fast, a little tight and I suspect a little pissed and he had hit the gate taking down about 6 feet of wall. The funny part was that I did not know that they taught officers to swear like that at Sandhurst.

There was an old local man who had just started work for the army and he worked in our compound doing odd jobs like mending furniture but his main drawback, or some might say his main advantage was that he could only speak a word or two of English. Now while this made life a little more difficult for him it gave us a chance to 'teach' him English. No not you're run of the mill ABC but more like army English. For example when you greet the CO it is an old English custom to say 'good morning you old bastard' and if the troop commander calls you then you say 'piss off' which means wait a minute, this sometimes got him into trouble and I might add us as well. Like the time we told him that in England we all like hot water and sugar and if he really wanted to get into troop commander's good books then that was the way to do it. Now please bear in mind that all this had to be relayed in sign language and Pidgin English, which only went to show how resourceful we were when we wanted to be. The troop commander called for his tea, old penis 'well that's what it sounded like' went in and left the hot water on his desk. It was about two minutes then he got that mad that it registered point five on the Richter scale. Now under the threat of a fate worse than death, old penis had no choice but to reveal the names of those men who in the eyes of the troop commander were traitors against the queen's commission. Now I would have not put it that strong although to be honest I did not mind cleaning the servicing pit of grease and oil as much as one or two of the other lads but I think what upset them was the fact that we also got three extra duties and we felt that it would be better had he shot us.

Very often out of a negative comes a positive and in this case old penis felt bad that he had grassed us up so as a treat he brought us some of his home made ouzo as a form of apology or maybe to get his own back on us, this stuff was very strong and nearly blew your bloody head off but with a bit of extra coke in it we still managed to drink it.

Next to our camp there was a camp of local military (I think they were Greek) and each morning they would wake up their men with a bugle call, now this was bloody annoying so one morning we all got up and started to throw mud and small stones at the bugler, this did not go down very well at all and he started to bellow for support and loads of soldiers came running out with their rifles and they started to cock their rifles and aimed them at us, now being heroic British soldiers we threw down our stones and ran back to our billet.

From time to time we had to go off for a few days detachment to some other unit. We all enjoyed this because most of the time it was a good skive and this time was no exception. Four of us set off with our trucks loaded up to the eyeballs with tents and poles; we got about halfway to our destination when I had to stop because of sheep on the road. Each truck slowed down and stopped each truck that is except Henry, who decided that he would buck the system and keep going.

Sadly there were three trucks in front of him but he had no intention of letting this stop him and he smashed into the back of the third truck and we all piled into each other.

When I ran back to see if he was ok, there was no sign of Henry, then we heard a soft moan coming from the cab and on closer inspection we found that he had slipped down near to the pedals and to be honest, that is what probably saved him from more serious injury.

Although Henry's truck was in a state it was ok to tow so being the hero of the group I said that I would tow him. After a couple of miles Henry was that bad that I stopped the truck and told him how to drive a truck that was on tow, after that he got better straight away and I never felt him again but that's not surprising as unknown to me the tow rope had broken about 4 miles back and

Henry was still there sat at the roadside thinking I had left him on purpose.

Another assignment was to go to the Swedish camp to take their officer to a village where there had been trouble between the 2 factions with lots of shooting going on, the Swedish soldiers that came with us were in 2 armoured personnel carriers and I drove their officer in an open top Land Rover, we stopped just outside of the village to make sure it was safe to enter and to be honest I was a little concerned.

What if they were shooting at each other while we were driving between them, "Don't worry" said the officer, "we are wearing blue berets so they won't shoot at us and my men are not worried" but then again, why should they be worried as they are sat in a bloody armoured personnel carrier (APC) while muggings here is in an open top vehicle, as it happened, there was no further shooting and my fears were totally unfounded although it did not feel like it at the time.

On our return to camp after that last detachment I went and collected my new suit from the on-site Taylor which I had just had made. It was my first made-to-measure suit and I was proud of it. I soon came down to earth after I showed it to the lads, 'that will be really nice when it's finished' said Titch and when I told them that it only cost £14 I knew that cold arse would make some sort of comment. 'For another couple of quid you could have had a new one' he said. I tried to bring the level of conversation up by showing them the short boxed shaped jacket, 'do you like the short jacket' I said. 'Your bum will get cold' said Titch, another friend of mine who we called rags, came into the billet. 'It's a pity there was not enough material to finish the jacket' he said, getting in on the act straight away, I sometimes wondered why I even bother to talk to this lot.

Christmas was fast approaching as was our time to go home and Fred started to call every aeroplane a GHM which means a going home machine.

Henry had been off driving for a few weeks but when we were getting a bit short of drivers Henry was sent out. That only lasted a couple of days then we got a call from an officer to say that if we ever sent that driver again, then we could not be held responsible for what he would do to him, and by now Henry had such a reputation as a Kami-Kasi driver that every time someone booked transport they asked the name of the driver and if Henry's name was given, the need for transport seemed to fade away.

Apart from a few men who were on duty over Christmas, we all had three days off.

We had a Christmas party in the cook-house which was terrible and the only thing that stopped it from dying was the fact that it turned into a rather chaotic vol au vent throwing competition which was made more interesting by the cooks who were fed up with the vol au vents being thrown so they decided to throw things themselves. These included things like plates, cups and anything else that they could lay their hands on, what jolly fun for the troops at Christmas.

Apart from finding Fred well pissed and trying to make love to a mop, the rest of Christmas went off without incident and straight after Christmas our thoughts were on returning home. We had been given the date and that was January 14th so we only had a couple of weeks to go. We all tried to keep it a secret from Henry in the hope he would miss the flight and be left in Cyprus but no such luck, some idiot told him.

We were informed that prior to leaving Cyprus we had to parade as a squadron to receive our UN medals for "Services to Peace" well that's what it says on the medal, we had to try and look our best which was rather difficult as we had no formal uniforms with us but parade we did and yes I still have the medal and wear it a couple of times each year for remembrance occasions, the weird part of the occasion was that I was only 18 when we went and was old enough to go on active service but we could not vote for which political party sent us there until we were 21.

We all spent a lot of time and money on presents for our loved ones, our wives or both. A lot of care was put into their selection, Titch bought his dad a good bottle of brandy, in fact he bought 4 bottles because each time he got one he drank it so had to go buy another one. So complete in our new suits, loaded to the ears with presents and yet again well pissed we set off on our journey home, and much to our delight, two weeks leave. Titch was to come to our house for a week, where it went a little wrong was when we decided to stop off for an hour to see some friends of my family and we sort of got involved in a party and by the time we left we were that pissed we fell asleep on the train and ended up missing the station and not arriving at my house until 1.30 in the morning. Matters were not made a lot better by the silly drunken comments being made by Titch, although I must add that my mother thought he was the best thing since sliced bread and over the years he got away with murder as I did whenever I stayed at his house.

On one occasion when Titch stayed with us we went out to the local pub called The Downham Tavern which on a Saturday night always had a live band playing and the band leader would try to encourage people up to sing, much the same happened in Salford in those pre karaoke days.

When Titch went to the toilet I told the band leader that we had a guest from Salford who was a great singer, so when he returned from the loo the band leader announced that we had a very special guest all the way from Salford and to be fair most of the audience had never heard of Salford, Titch smiled and was looking round for this special guest until his name was announced, he did not know what to do but with encouragement from the audience he got up and started to sing "Are you lonesome tonight" well, he was pretty bad and to save the day 2 old ladies went on the stage and helped him and the audience loved it.

According to our CO the time we spent in Cyprus was just a holiday and it was now time to get down to some work. A holiday!!! God it was active service and I have a medal to prove it. How can it be called a holiday when there was no ice for the drinks, but work we did, with only the odd incident to help overcome the boredom. One day I was helping to work on a truck in the workshop and because it was bitter cold we had the roller shutters down to try to keep the place warm. Well it got a lot warmer when the welder shouted that he had a blowback.

Now I thought that this meant that he had something wrong with his bowels but when I saw everyone running I decided that being a super hero was not for me and that the best course of action was to be like the rest and run, but as I said the roller shutters were down and an old sergeant with a limp was trying to get the doors open enough so that he could get out but every time he got them up for a few feet the rest of us would pile through. I went under the shutter with such speed that I almost welded my gaiters to my ankle. Cold arse said that the last time that he had seen me moving that fast was when I was trying to get out of the pub without buying my round.

As soon as we got out of the workshop we dived into the nearest shelter which just happened to be the coal bunker, we only just made it before the whole roof went up in a very loud bang and a bigger cloud of dust and most of that dust seemed to come from the bloody coal bunker and after a safe period of time we came out looking like we had been in the oven on a high gas for a couple of hours. The result of all this was that the workshop had no roof.

I had no pride and the CO had no sympathy and we ended up working all hours that God sent trying to find as many pieces of truck as we could.

It was at this time in my life I was learning the art of survival in the army and every day I was learning something new.

We were a working unit and each week one of us had to do what was known as the "Milk Run" which meant picking up goods from some depots and then delivering our load to various camps around the country and we would be away for most of the week but in those days if you were driving for more than 5 hours you got a plus 5 allowance so most of us enjoyed the Milk Run because it earned you extra money.

Another rather difficult job that I had was to take a wooden mock-up of a tank on the back of a flatbed 3 tonner from Catterick to Inverness in Scotland to the Black Watch and I assume that it was used on the range as a target.

It was a long and arduous drive and when I arrived at the barracks there was a guard on duty in full uniform and a kilt and sporran and the looked magnificent, "Evening Jock" I said where can I park this up for the night, don't f***ing call me Jock he said in a broad London accent, now this did throw me for a bit but was later told that during the war they were allowed to recruit in London and some of the lads wanted to join the same regiment as their father or grandfather, how true that was I do not know but it satisfied me at the time.

It was about this time in March 1967 that a large ship called the Torrey Canyon decided that it would sink and spew out its cargo of oil.

Then some bright spark in London, either a politician or some half pissed general decided that it would be a good idea to bomb the bloody ship (you can almost hear them in the bar saying this) and that way the oil will catch light and will not reach the beaches, yes ok, time to leave the bar!! Because they did bomb the ship and all of the oil did not catch light and most of the bloody oil went onto the beaches of the south west coast of England. We were called in to transport detergent from regional depots to the beaches where soldiers of the infantry would use it to try and keep the beaches and surrounding areas free from oil.

We were posted all around the South West and a few of us were stationed in the TA Barracks in St Ives in Cornwall which is a beautiful town with lovely people but the barracks were not a very comfortable place to spend 6 weeks and often we would sleep in our trucks but the plus side of getting up early and getting on the road was that after we had gone to the depot and collected our load, on the way back we would stop at a café for breakfast and the owner always gave the soldiers a free breakfast.

It did not take long for even the slowest of soldiers to realise that here was a chance to make a few bob. Fisherman were buying the detergent to clean the oil off their boats, at £5 for a 45 gallon drum, farmers were buying the empty drums, which for the soldiers were very easy to come by, for £2 each. Fishermen were also the best buyers of the heavy oil skins that were provided to protect our clothes from the detergent.

They were sold for £5 a set which I thought was very good value for the money. There were more fiddles here than the London Philharmonic with most of the people involved earning more on the side than from their wages.

We worked very hard for the time that we were in the West Country but the infantry worked even harder as their work was very manual but our was just sitting in a truck and getting the detergent to them to contain the damage done by the oil and in some places this was very hard to do as there were rocks leading to beaches that were all covered in oil so the infantry used large hoses and generators to pump the detergent too hard to reach areas, now it took two men to hold the hose when it was operating as the pressure was huge but on this particular occasion the sergeant in charge of the section was not a very nice guy and was hated by most of his men, so when he rapped the hose around his arm (with the generator not on) and started to climb over the rocks, his men had other ideas and when he was half way down someone (never did find out who) turned on the generator and the sergeant just flew up into the air and then landed on the rocks, so all work had to stop while an ambulance was called and he was evacuated to hospital and his section then got on with the job and although I did not see him with his section again I do not know what happened to him.

We were given the odd night off to go out and on this occasion there was a dance going on in Penzance and they laid on a truck to take us there and ensure that we got back ok.

When we arrived one of the lads noticed that the "Barley Wine" was very cheap so we started to drink it very fast and of course, it was not long until we were all shitfaced.

Now as a responsible soldier (ok, so that may not be true) I thought that rather than crash out on the dance floor I would go and crash out in the back of the truck that was going to take us back.

When I got to the car park there were 4 trucks and I knew which was one was ours but unfortunately by the time I got to the rear of the trucks I got into the wrong one and it was the one that was going to be parked there all night which I found out at about 5 in the morning when I woke up, I decided that the best course of action would be to go to the local police station to see if I could get a lift but the desk sergeant was very blunt and totally unsympathetic to my problem and suggested that I get onto the main road and try to hitch a lift, thanks for your help!!!

As I left the police station another officer came out to direct me to the main road and told me to just walk up that road, a few minutes later the same policeman came along and gave me a lift back to base, what a nice bloke.

We were down there a total of 6 weeks and when we returned to Catterick there were an awful lot of new cars and new clothes floating about and the standard story was that the poor little souls had been working that hard that they hadn't been able to spend their pennies so they saved them.

Now if you believe that then you would believe that Henry went the whole 6 weeks without an accident and alas that was not so, but I did buy a Wolsley 8/80 on our return and it was an ex London police car complete with the gap where there used to be a police bell for those of you old enough to remember.

The West of England were not ready for this human tornado called Henry and to be fair, Henry was not ready for the west of England. Its narrow winding roads confused the poor bloke and it was not long before his reputation was known throughout the west and the Sunday driver almost became the thing of the past. Nothing was safe, farm gates, tractors, parked motorcycles, anything.

Henry spent that much time bashing the dents in and that much time bashing the dents out that I think he must have been one of the few who made no money on the side at all.

Chapter Four

Off to Germany

It was about this time that we had a rather major scare, it was when things were not going well in the Middle East and a few blokes got killed and it was decided that there may be a need for more troops and we were put on standby. Now we all felt that this was a rather dirty trick, I mean, we had not joined the army to fight or anything nasty like that. I was allergic to fighting and whenever I came into contact with physical violence I broke out in cuts and bruises and none of us relished the thought of getting hit by a whoosh-bang- oh-nasty (a bullet) and we were rather low for a few days, we perked up a lot when we were told that the crisis had blown over and we were not needed and in fact this was the occasion that a CO nicknamed mad Mike led his men into an area called Crater, in Aden and rescued one of his companies and later became a member of parliament.

Also around that time there were a few areas in the middle east that were experiencing troubles in their region and on one occasion we had to go up north to an ammunition depot, load our trucks and then drive down to Harwich where our trucks were unloaded onto ships, now this went on for two weeks so we had learner drivers from another regiment in Catterick who would drive up north then we would take over and drive down to the port with a full load of ammunition and then they would drive back to Catterick and we would sleep, where they finished and we then got new learners and repeated the whole process again.

On one return trip we were in convoy when one of the trucks full of ammunition came off the road (no, I don't think it was Henry driving) we all stopped and a very young officer suggested that one of us e.g. me, get on to the truck to check that all was ok with the ammunition, now there are times in the army when officers should take the lead and this is one of those times so I suggested that maybe it would look better if he went and checked it and of course the OC would be impressed.

By this time going on exercise was no great problem because we had now learned how to live in comfort while on exercise and we had also learned the art of skiving and in the summer going on exercise could also be a lot of fun.

On another occasion we were sent to Scotland to support a company of Italian Alpine troops and transport them to and support them on the Isle of Skye, what a beautiful place with lovely people but in those days there was no bridge across the water and you had to get a ferry which did make it a bit insular and cut off from the mainland, we had so much fun but what I did find strange was the fact that pubs were not allowed to open on a Sunday but hotels were allowed to open and it very soon became obvious that a pub which was known as the George and Dragon was, if you looked at the signage closely the George and Dragon hotel as they had a couple of rooms that they could let out although I am not sure if any of them ever did.

The church in Portree was dead opposite the pub (sorry, hotel) and when the church service was over and everyone was leaving they came out of the church in two lines, women and children were in one line and as they emerged they went home for the wives to prepare Sunday lunch while the other line was all men and they headed straight across the road for a drink and remember back in the 60's they only opened from 12 to 2pm so they had to get out of the church and start drinking very quickly.

We were billeted in the local TA hall very close to the town centre of Portree and would walk down there most evening as we were there for a couple of weeks and made lots of friends with the local girls.

The major in charge of the whole operation was an ex SAS officer and was a decent bloke apart from the time when I drove him to a mountain (ok, it may have been a very large steep hill) with the Italians and he asked if I had ever climbed and when I answered no I am sure I saw a twinkle in his eye and a smile when he said that we, as

British soldiers should show the Italians that we can adapt and when we arrived he put a rope around my waist and just pulled me up the mountain (ok, Hill) and we ended up beating them to the top but I am sure that the shit was running down my leg but it did make a great story in the pub that night although you would be forgiven in thinking that I had just climbed Mount Everest.

We were invited to a dance in the local church hall and we were also informed that no alcohol was allowed so we all took bottles of various soft drinks which I should add were doctored slightly with whisky, rum or brandy but the more pissed we got the braver we got and when all the girls asked us all to dance we were happy to try this out, especially as we started in a big circle but then one of the couple go into the centre of the circle, prance about for a bit and the gently pull your partner across the floor back to the edge of the circle, now I forget what this dance was called by other but to me it was pure torture and purgatory as the girl I was partnered with was a very big girl with muscles like Charles Atlas (I think she may have done his course) and she must have forgot about the gentle bit and she in fact threw me across the dance floor and I almost left the room, that my friends was the last time I tried Scottish dancing.

Now back in Yorkshire we also had other duties such as duty driver and in the winter there was a huge amount of snow, which was most winters in Yorkshire and on one particular duty we had a call from the hospital to say that an ambulance going to collect a women who was about to have her baby, had gone off the road in the ice and would it be possible for a long wheel base land rover to go into the middle of nowhere to her home to pick her up and take her to the hospital.

Myself and another young single man went off to collect her and with her husband transport them to the hospital and I must tell you that trying to drive in thick snow and ice in the countryside with two hysterical men shouting rather loudly, "take deep breaths, do not push oh shit I can see the head" now this is a great incentive to go faster and we managed to arrive at the hospital in time for the nice couple to have their baby delivered by a doctor who knew what they were doing rather than two young duty drivers, believe me, that was the last thing we wanted to deliver.

It was early the following year that there were horrific gales in Glasgow and again our squadron went up there with a huge amount of tarpaulins to help as many roofs were blown away but the good news for me was that 5 of us did not have to go as we were about to be posted to Germany.

I got a posting to Bielefeld in Germany. There was 5 of us in the draft and to be honest I was looking forward to going and it was on a cold day in February that we arrived to start our tour of Germany.

We had been there an hour when we found out that there was a pub just outside the back gate. Well it was our duty to investigate this so we decided to visit the place. Now we had been in Germany about 5 hours by the time we ventured out of the back gate in search of this pub. What people failed to inform us about was the fact that they drive on the other side of the road out there. We went out of the back gate and looked to our right to see if there was anything coming, we were just about to cross when a bloody great lorry almost hit us, 'he must be pissed' said Nobby and then we all realised that it was us who were wrong.

The great thing about Bielefeld was that most of the lads there were very young and all we ever wanted to do was have fun and we did almost every day. I had not been there long when the troop sergeant asked me if I would like to go on a trip to Norway. Well, being young and stupid I did not see the sparkle in his eyes. I accepted and he went off with a smile on his face and singing at the top of his voice. A couple of weeks later I found out why he was so happy, this little trip to Norway was in fact an Army Outward Bound Course and the troop sergeant had been trying for months to con some poor pillock into volunteering but there was nobody that stupid until he found me!!!

I found out after a few days that others had gone on this course and not made the finish and in fact nobody from our regiment had ever passed this course and one of our corporals, I will call him Harris, was as fit as a butchers dog and he had muscles on top of muscles, this man used to go for a 5 mile run before breakfast and he failed the Outward Bound Course, now what chance for little skinny wimpy me I asked and when I asked, most of the lads fell about laughing because they were thinking the same.

To go on this course you had to be able to swim at least 50 yards and I was almost a non-swimmer. Now I thought that this may help me to get off the course but when I saw the troop sergeant about it all he said was that any soldier worth his salt could learn to swim in 4 weeks and it would not take a lot more effort to swim 50 yards wearing overalls.

'You said nothing about overalls' I said, 'well I did not want to put you off' he said. There are times when I feel a bit like a mushroom, always kept in the dark and often dropped in the shit.

The task of teaching me to swim was given to a friend of mine called Scouse and he made a good job of it. Three days before I was due to go on the course I was ready to do my swimming test, two lengths in the pool wearing a pair of overalls, it was about 7.30 in the morning and it was bloody freezing.

The sergeant major had come in early to test me and because he was on a special parade later that morning he was wearing his best kit. 'Ok young man, off you go' he said. Now the first length was not that hard but by the time I started the second length the overalls were full of water and i was finding it very hard to lift my arms out of the water. Now before some smart arse says why did you not do breast stroke, it was because I did not know how to do it as I had only been taught how to crawl and by this time can assure you that it was a crawl in fact I was only just about moving.

This worried the sergeant major, not because he thought that I may drown but he thought that he might have to jump in to pull me out. The very thought of his best boots and razor edge creases coming into contact with the swimming pool made him very resourceful, 'swim you bastard swim' he bellowed and I did the last few yards in record breaking time and as the sergeant major turned to go I swear that I saw him sweating.

To get to the course was a challenge in itself as I had to go by train from Bielefeld and when on the train I met loads of other young stupid soldiers who had also volunteered for the course, the train went through part of Germany, then through Denmark and then we had to catch a ferry across to Kristiansand in Norway, where we were met by the course staff and loaded onto 3 ton trucks for the trip to the Outward Bound Centre, I believe that there were about 60 of us and all in all it was a long and tiring journey and there were troops from all over Germany and we even had a Canadian but I was not aware that there were any Canadians stationed in Germany.

The course was to say the least very interesting and it started the moment the truck arrived at the Outward Bound Centre.

What a shock we all had when we were told to get off the truck and change into pajamas. 'Oh good we are all going to bed' said one wit, we were all then told to line up by the foreshore a funny place for a sleep I thought but was soon put straight. 'What's your name' said a corporal who looked like a cross between a gorilla and an Irish Wolfhound and not wishing to offend the gentleman, I told him my name 'how far can you swim' he said in a tone that would turn beer flat, 'Fifty yards but only just' I said 'ok swim out to that first boat' he said with another sneer across his face. It looked to be about 15 yards away, this will be a doddle I thought and I made it pretty easy but as I was just about to get hold of the boat the man inside got rather ratty and hit my hand with the oar. 'Swim to the next boat' he said and I did but this one was a lot further and I only just made it. 'Don't you dare touch this bloody boat or I will shove this oar right up your arse' said the gentleman inside, "swim to the shore"

Now having no wish to end up looking like a shish kebab this was a threat that I could not ignore so being a good lad I continued swimming towards the shore and I don't know how I found the strength to get there but get there I did and as I was crawling up the beach an instructor came along.

'How far did you say you could swim?' he said 'fifty yards only just' I panted sounding rather like a set of antique bellows. 'Well you have just done about 100 yards so you are improving' he said as he walked away with a spring in his stride, cocky bastard I thought, hope his bloody canoe sinks.

We were to spend 3 weeks by the sea and then 3 weeks up in the mountains so we had 6 weeks of torture to endure.

The rules of the course were very simple, you had various tasks to do each and every day but you did not have to do them and you were always given the chance to refuse to do that task but that meant that you failed the course and were returned to your unit straight away (RTU) and many of the guys, for various reasons decided that it was not for them.

On the first morning we all had to get on parade in 2 lines, about 30 men in each line and squat down with our arms on each other's shoulders and they then laid what can only be described as a telegraph poll on our arms and we then had to bunny hop as a group up a hill holding this bloody great poll on our arms, I must say that it was for only a short but very difficult distance and felt like hell and the next morning a few of the lads dropped out rather than do it again.

On another morning we went for a run and on our return we took a diversion very near to the camp, we were told to form a line and those of us that were near the rear of the group after the run wondered what was going on when a number of the guys came back and said that were not doing that!!!

One of the instructors came back and told us that we were to jump off the side into the water below and when we asked him how high that was he just smiled and suggested that we did not creep up to the edge and have a look, as many of those that refused had done but run straight out and then look down as you could not then refuse, when I did the jump it was not as bad as I thought it would be and after that we did it a few times but I am sure that if the lads that refused were allowed to speak to one of us that had completed it then they may have had a go.

Another skill that we learnt was to Kayak, now bear in mind that I was a city boy and although as a young lad we used to play by the water in the Thames that was about the limit to our water based skills now some instructor was trying to be patient and teach us how to paddle a Kayak as this was in preparation for a 2 day expedition into the Baltic.

We had to learn how to get out of the Kayak if it capsized or to stay in the Kayak and get it back upright again without leaving the Kayak, oh what fun we had!!!!!

All of the Kayaks were doubles and I was doubled up with a Scottish lad, yes, you are right, his name was Jock and he was a great laugh.

The expedition started with us paddling some distance into the Baltic Sea and it was not long before we were strung out for most of the Baltic with the instructors not very impressed but we did eventually get to our destination which was a small rock strewn island where we would be spending the night but we were given some fishing lines and matches to light a fire and we were very lucky as Jock and I managed to catch 2 fish which we cooked on an open fire and enjoyed but we were both from city's so we were not versed in the rules or ways of the countryside.

On our return to the Outward Bound Centre we had a de-brief regarding the whole exercise and each pair were asked for their opinions on how it all went, when it came to our turn the instructor asked us if we managed to catch any fish and it was with great pride the we declared that we had caught 2 and we ate and enjoyed them, the instructor was very impressed "and how did you gut them" he asked, at this point both Jock and I just looked at each other, er "what do you mean" said I and the whole group fell about laughing.

We had no idea that you had to take the guts out of the fish before eating it, so we ate the whole thing although we did admit that the bones were a bit of a problem but that was all and we had no side effects at all from eating the guts of a fish.

One of our mates was taken to hospital after some sort of accident and we were allowed an afternoon to go into Kristiansand Hospital to see him, well actually we spent very little time with him but more time chatting up the nurses who seemed to find us all very interesting because nobody really knew what went on at the course but every now and again somebody would get injured and taken to the hospital.

I found out later that the swimming was the easy part of the course and to be honest I was not looking forward to the second part of the course which was up in the mountains and consisted of various mountain type activities, one of which was the one day march. Now this was ideal for any young masochist but to anyone with about an ounce of brain power it was pure torture. Just before lunch we had to cross a rather high crumbly hill. Now this was difficult enough on its own but in my case it was made more difficult the young Scottish lad who had been my partner on the Baltic exercise and who insisted on telling me a string of jokes.

Most of his jokes I had heard before but every now and then he would tell a good one, it was pure bad luck that the moment he told the best joke was just as I was about to cross a rather difficult gap. As I went across the gap he came to the punch line, I laughed, I slipped and then I fell sliding all the way down the hill on my arse.

When I reached the bottom I came to a crushing halt just by the side of the road, at that moment the OC's Landover came round the bend, out jumped the OC 'are you ok young man?' he said, 'what happened?' 'Well sir my rucksack fell down the mountain" I said 'but unfortunately I was still wearing it at the time'. I don't think the poor man ever did understand me.

As we did each task more and more men dropped out and were returned to unit but the teams remained the same, so some teams had 8 men while other teams had only 3 or 4 men, now this meant that if we were in competition in any way then each man in the team with 4 men had to do the task twice.

As we were nearing the end of the course we had to compete in a race which went a few hundred yards down the track, round a very large boulder, where you could not be seen by the rest of the teams or the instructors and then return to the start with 2 teams going at the same time and when you got to the boulder you went different ways around it, now our team was down to 4 men and I had already been round once but I had to go again.

This time I was up against a very fresh, fit and muscle bound Canadian who could have ate me for breakfast and the worst thing was that the team that lost this race were to clean the toilets for the remainder of the course.

This was a relay race and by the time my team mate had got back the big Canadian was well in front and by the time I started to go round the boulder he came by with a big smile on his face as he knew he would easily beat me but he had not taken into consideration that I was a cheating little bastard who did not want to clean the toilets so as he passed me at great speed, I put out my foot and tripped him up but as he fell he went down the side of the hill!!!! As I came into sight from the boulder I was greeted with great cheers and great surprise and when asked where was the other guy I said I thought I saw him slip and fall down the hill it was only on his return when he wanted to kill me that the story came out but to my delight, the result stood and the other team cleaned the toilets, oh bliss.

At the end of the course there were only 13 of us who had passed the course, all of the others had either failed a task or refused to do a task but out of the 13 most of us had some sort of injury to arms or legs so we did look a bit of a motley crew on the train journey back to Germany and I was very proud to be the first member of that regiment to have passed the very tough Army Outward Bound Course.

After returning from the torture that is called an Outward–Bound Course I got involved in the football team which always seemed to have a good time whenever they went away to matches. One story I must tell in fact happened just before my arrival. The team were in the quarter final of the cup and they had to travel all the way to Berlin.

Now when they arrived on the Friday evening the lads of course wanted to go and have a look round the town but were told to be in early because of the match the next day.

Now that was a bit like leaving a child alone in a sweet shop and not expecting them to try some and they did but the problem was that most of the team tried too much and just before kick-off time they were still three parts pissed.

What made matters worse was the fact that the star centre forward was having trouble with his piles and they came down. Now the messy and rather rotten job of putting them back fell to the team manager who spent the next 90 minutes spewing all over the place and did not see any of the match anyway, so with something coming down and something coming up we were very lucky to have won the game 2-1.

There was so much going on in and around the camp that you were never bored and being a bit young and stupid I volunteered for anything that was going.

One of those things was a snow survival course in the Hartz mountains, now please do not ask me why I volunteered as I had never skied before but it seemed like a good idea at the time and to be honest I enjoyed most of it including making and sleeping in an igloo for a night but my course came to an end when trying to ski rather fast down a hill I went over and the rifle that was slung over my shoulder came round and out of spite, smacked me over the head, knocking me out for a short time but when I started to throw up they thought it may be time to get me off to hospital and although I had mild concussion they would not let me re-join the course for the last couple of days.

I also tried many other sports which included volunteering for the boxing team, now this only came about when I saw that the team used to get special meals which included very large lovely looking steaks while the rest of us only managed to get the rough old steak, as anyone who knows me will tell you I am not the fighting sort and I am afraid that my boxing career came to a halt when I realised that it hurt when someone punched you in the face and I had no intention to ruin my boyish good looks!!!

I then tried cricket but to be honest I did get rather bored stood way out in a part of a field with nobody to talk to so I just started daydreaming which was ok until I heard the rest of the team yelling at me and the ball landed right in front of me and I thought that was really good until someone explained that they wanted me to catch the bloody ball.

They did not give up on me and they then tried me at batting which lasted for 1 ball and I was out for LBW (leg before wicket) so I felt that maybe I was not cut out for cricket, now I know what you are thinking, were you any bloody good at any sports and it turned out that yes I was.

As a young soldier I enjoyed most physical activity and yes that did diminish over the years but some I enjoyed more than others and one of those was the cross country running team which I was ok at but found it very hard work and hard work for me was a very dirty word so I only competed a few times and then moved on to the Volkslauf, which was cross country speed walking and I found that I was very good at that and the fact that training took place early in the day meant that we missed early morning parades which was great.

We entered competitions all over Germany and Holland over a distance of between 6 and 10km's and won loads of medals but also had loads of fun which included one of our officers, who really wanted to break the course record at one event, sitting in the back of a land rover shaking a case of beer to keep us going for the last kilometer and it worked as we did break the record.

Of course, we still had work and exercises to complete and do remember that sport was not part of our work although we did manage to get away with a lot of things because of sport.

There was a training area near to us which used to welcome TA unit from all over the UK for their annual training exercises and we picked them and their equipment up from the RAF airport and brought them to the training area and we would then be used as transport support for the next 2 weeks and to be honest, for us it was a very cushy job, now the first unit was from Yorkshire and when I came out of my tent in the morning there was a TA soldier looking at me and it was like looking in a mirror, bloody hell and as the day went on and the other lads started to notice they started to call us brothers and everywhere we went over the 2 week period people thought that we were brothers and there was a time when I wondered if his father had been from or lived in London but then I heard his surname which sounded Polish and it was as his dad was Polish, they were a nice bunch of lads and on the day they went back we picked up the next group who were from Wales.

I had been to Wales on a couple of occasions as I said earlier but I found it very difficult to understand their accents but we did get on very well and it only took a couple of days before they were trying to teach me some Welsh songs such as Sospan Fach (pronounced Vach) and there was another one which was asking "why do we have an English prince of Wales" and for many years later my Welsh friends were rather surprised that the common old Londoner knew some of their songs.

I had not been at Bielefeld long when together with a couple of other guys we had to take some officers on a recce to the Belgian border, this was deemed to be a good cushy number as we only had to drive them around for a few hours and then we went back to a very nice hotel for our meals which were all paid for by the army, it was also the first time I had stayed in a hotel and the first time that I saw a duvet as we had only ever had sheets and blankets and of course, overcoats on top of the bed in winter when I was young.

In November 1968 I, at last, became an adult because in those day the coming of age was 21 and it was only then that you were allowed to vote, so it was a big celebration to get to "Adulthood" and all of the lads got together and organised a party for my birthday and wow was it a party and as they paid for all of the drinks and the buffet it was even better but as I said earlier, you were old enough to go on active service but you were not old enough to vote for who sent you on active service until after your 21st birthday.

As a young teenager I had joined the Army cadets and an adult instructor know as Q became friends with the family and he encouraged my mother to let me start training for a massive event held in Holland every August called the Nijmegen marches and to ensure that we were in good shape we had a training day marching over the Romney Marshes in Kent wearing gas masks and gas capes, apparently this was to ensure that we could cope with the hot summer sun in Holland in August but it was all to no avail as I became ill and could not go but life was about to take a funny turn!!

In Bielefeld we had a Squadron Sergeant Major who was Polish and a great man, he seemed to encourage all of the younger soldiers and convinced them that they could do anything if they put their mind to it and that was when the event of Nijmegen came up again as K (as he was known behind his back) was trying to get a team to enter the military category and yes you are right, I did volunteer for it as I had always wanted to do it and ended up doing it 5 times in all but that first time was an eye opener because when we got to Holland all military personnel were in a tented camp and it was massive but the thing that got my attention most was the "thunder boxes" or toilets as most people call them but these were about twenty yards long and seating for about 20 soldiers, ok I may be exaggerating a little but there was only a partial curtain between you and the next bloke so you were sat there having a dump and chatting about the day's activity at the same time.

The other thing that also shocked me was we had stopped for a short break on the first day and all of a sudden this rather loud voice said "that's young Keith" and when I turned round it was Q from my army cadet days and who was still training young cadets in the same way as he did us.

I had done the march that year, got my medal and as far as I was concerned at the end of the day I had done what I set out to do and did not want to volunteer the following year so when all the team were doing training I was not part of the team and about 3 weeks before the marches I went on a kayaking exercise for a couple of weeks.

On my return to camp K came to see me and informed me that 2 men were injured and could not go to Holland and they only had one reserve but unless they could find another volunteer before the week-end the whole team would have to withdraw, he was a master of the sad story and I found myself saying yes even though I knew that it was going to be the hardest march as after 2 weeks of my feet being in water they were too soft to withstand marching for about a 130 miles and so it turned out.

After day 3 of 4 my feet were severely blistered and I was not sure if I could make it on the last day but after an encouragement talk from K I decided I would try to complete it or we would not get the team medal.

It was about 6 miles from the end and I had dropped behind the main group and my feet were wet with blood and I thought sod it, what am I doing this for so I sat on the edge of the road and removed my boots and counted 26 blisters on my feet, so I thought I had a good enough reason to give up and I was sat there just waiting for the "Knacker

Wagon" to come along and pick me up, however, at that point along came a Dutch man and sat beside me and said "you British are so very brave, your feet are full of blisters and there is blood everywhere but you British do not give up" oh shit, what could I do but start to put my boots back on and he then requested if he could walk with me as it would give him strength, and yes I did finish the march.

Life in Bielefeld was not all about sports although it did seem like it at times, we had a cinema in the camp and they were showing "Jungle Book" starting that day, now me and a mate of mine decided we would like to see the film so we went to the cinema and there was a very long queue and what was worse was that any adult in the queue had a child with them and it would look very strange if 2 adult soldier were in the queue on their own, we looked at each other and then from nowhere came a great idea from me.

I had a mate who was married with a young son and he only lived a couple of minutes away so we went to his house and explained our situation and asked if we could borrow his young son and treat him to the cinema and we will throw in an ice cream as well, the son knew me well as I used to babysit for him so he was delighted to take up our offer and his parents agreed and so we went and watched jungle book, we all enjoyed it.

A friend of mine, scouse, was getting married to a young WRAC soldier and I was highly chuffed when he asked me to be his best man and he was getting married in the catholic church in another camp just down the road but to be honest the catholic padre was not a great bloke, he thought that he could control all of his congregation, so when we went for a couple of rehearsals he kept warning us about having a stag night where you got totally shit faced and told us that if the groom came to his church still pissed he would not marry them, now we had to take this on board as scouse's mum had travelled from England for the wedding.

On the evening prior to the wedding we decided that having taken notice of the padre, we would go out for a stag do but would not go overboard and would make an effort to be back and in bed by about 11pm,I am sure you know where this is going, we eventually got back by about 5am and scouse was out of his head and the wedding was at 10am but we had to get there by about 09.30, now this presented a huge challenge to us but by golly we were RCT and we could rise to this challenge.

3 of us managed to get him undressed and into the shower, this was not easy as he

found it very difficult to stand up and all he wanted to do was go to sleep so a different approach was required, turn the water on to cold and it was bloody freezing so we could not leave him there for long, so we got him out of the shower and started filling him up with black coffee and about 4 hours later he was sober enough to convince the padre that he was ok and had been sensible the night before !!!

At the reception his mother made a point of thanking me for not getting him pissed out of his head and for looking after him and ensuring that he was sober enough to get married to his lovely wife, wow that was close.

Chapter Five

Parachuting and fun

Both K and my mate scouse had both been in the parachute regiment and there was also an ex SAS man in HQ and they decided that our regiment should enter a team in a competition called "Parashot" which was in 2 very different parts, the first part was a parachute jump from a small aircraft called a Lysander and you had to land as close as possible to a target on the ground and then part 2 was a military skills test and entailed a rifle range and other skills such as avoiding an ambush, this all very interesting until I was told that each team had to have 4 people, 3 plus a reserve, now I am sure that you know which way this is going but I did not realise for some time that the three of them were being very nice and civil to me which was not like scouse at all and finally they asked me to be part of the team and although I was happy to volunteer yet again, there was one minor point I was not sure about and that was, I was not ex parachute regiment and had never jumped out of a plane and as that was part of the competition I wondered how this would work.

I should have known that they had already worked that one out and they had found that at a military grass airstrip not far away they held free fall parachute courses but you had to pay to go on them, great, that was my way out but no, they had already ensured that the regiments would pay for the course, oh how nice of them !!!

So off I went on the free fall course not knowing what to expect and I found a number of other young men on the course and I became friends with a Scotsman and yes you are right, his name was jock, now can you see a pattern emerging here as I always seem to mate up with a Scotsman and we also met the chief instructor called Bob A and when he left the army I believe that he opened a prisoner of war camp in Scotland where he charged large companies a lot of money to send their employees on team building weekends at his camp and as far as I am aware it was a successful venture.

The first few days were spent in the classroom learning the theory of jumping out of an aircraft and very importantly we also spent a lot of time learning how to pack a parachute, this became more important when we learnt that we would all be packing our own parachutes for all jumps, all of a sudden we paid a lot more attention.

The aircraft that was being used was called a De-Havilland Rapide, this was a twin winged wooden aircraft and when we were shown round we found out that we would have to climb onto the wing before jumping backwards off the aircraft, that sounds like fun we thought (not)

The morning of our first jump was full of trepidation, fear, anxiety and every other emotion you can think of but we all put on our jump suits, our main chute and our emergency chute and a very nervous 4 blokes headed towards the aircraft.

Bob A was the jumpmaster and he had to run through a few safety point before boarding and just to put us at ease he then told us that in the event of both the main chute and the emergency chute failing to open we should then put our arms out straight to the side and cross our right leg over our left leg, he pointed out that this would not stop us getting killed but would mean that they could get us out of the ground on a left hand thread, what a laugh he was, just what we needed to calm the nerves.

That first jump was from 2.500 feet and was a static line jump and anyone who has done a free fall course will know that first jump is not the worst as you do not know what is happening and what to expect but by the second jump you do know and that is a lot worse.

It was now my turn and the jumpmaster indicated that I should move by the door and then he instructed me to get onto the wing then I should have felt a dig in the ribs which meant go but I seemed to be there for some time and when I looked in to the aircraft the jumpmaster was indicating that

I should go back into the aircraft which I did but by this time I was glad that I was wearing the brown trouser under my jumpsuit, I then had to wait for the aircraft to make another circuit and then got onto the wing and this time I did feel the dig in the ribs and jumped into the unknown.

The actual jump was a fantastic experience although the build up to the jump could have been better and when the aircraft landed the jumpmaster told me that the reason he called me back into the aircraft was the static line had caught over the buckle on my harness and although this would have made no difference to the chute opening it would have spun me round and made my first jump very scary, yer ok.

We were all full of adrenalin and could not stop talking and telling each other how bloody brave we had all been and then it was time to get changed and go into the club to get de-briefed, have our first entry in our log book signed and to have a beer or maybe more than one and it was at this time we learnt about "Dead Ants" yes this may seem very strange but whenever we got together or if the weather was too bad to jump we would end up in the club house having a beer or two and playing the game !!

I am sure that this still goes on in loads of parachute clubs all over the country although now days it may be called something else.

Dead Ants, we will start with the Ant bowl and in our club this was a huge bowl which I suspect started life as an ice bucket, now the Ant bowl is filled with beer and is passed around the bar and the loser has to pay for the beer but they then become the Ant master and when he shouted Dead Ants you had to get onto the floor as quickly as possible.

You then lay on your back with your arms and legs in the air and you had to stay like that until the Ant master has decided who was last and the loser and you could all then get up, finish any beer that was left in the Ant bowl and when the new Ant master is ready, which can be at any time, he can call Dead Ants and this can go on all evening or all day if you start early enough.

Now when the Ant bowl starts to come round some of the lads may add to the bowl, no, not beer but by putting their sock or underpants into the bowl and nobody was allowed to remove them before the end of the session.

Now on one occasion, I think it may have been at the end of the course, you could invite family and friends to join us in the club and no they were not required to partake in the game but the game did continue and one of the people on the course was a young officer whose father was a serving colonel and he invited both his mother and father to the end of course party and it was not long before the Ant bowl started the rounds and we were telling his parents about the game and the various thing that people put in the Ant bowl when it came to us and as the young officer started to drink from the bowl a very large sock very slowly slid down the side of his face but the funniest part was looking at his mother's face, I thought that she was going to throw up but the best part was when he explained to his mother how lucky he was as he had noticed some grubby underpants in the bowl and they missed his face.

There were many great laughs at the parachute club some made us laugh and some made the locals laugh as at the week-end we would have many local families bring their children to the airstrip to see the parachutists and on one occasion there seemed to be more people than usual and the wind was a little unpredictable as it seemed to gust as and when it wanted which is not great when you are trying to land as close as possible to the ground target.

I had made a very normal jump and as I approach the drop zone (DZ) at about 200 feet I turned into the wind which helps to slow you down ready for landing but the wind dropped and I was in danger of going into the crowd of locals so I then decided to turn so that the wind was behind me so that I would miss both the crowd and the fence they were standing by, unfortunately at this point the wind dropped to almost nothing and I fell to earth in a rather undignified way but as this drop in wind caught me out I landed in a very awkward way and as I stood up I was in a great deal of pain.

Although I was in pain and as the crowd had been so nice and in fact they had all clapped and cheered when I landed I felt I had to pull in my parachute, smile and thank the crowd and walk back to the club without showing any signs of injury, but I was in agony and it turned out that I had broken a toe but it did not stop me from jumping.

Free fall parachuting can be exhilarating and a great deal of fun but of course there are always times when things can and do go wrong but I must stress that this is not often.

As far as I can remember I did not know of any incident where someone had to deploy their emergency parachute, although I did come close once myself.

Everything was ok until the parachute deployed and I then knew immediately that something was wrong as I could not put my head up straight and when I looked sideways I could see that the lines were twisted and I needed to kick in one direction to start the process to unravel them but as it started to unravel I started to kick in the opposite direction or I would have had yet another problem but I did not think that this was anything bad until I had finally unraveled the cord and I felt the parachute pull and I could hear people clapping and cheering and when I looked down I was only about 200 feet from the ground and I had not realised how fast I was falling.

My friend Jock was with the Kings Own Scottish Borderers or the KOSB as they were known as and he had driven to the course in a Volkswagen Karmann Ghia but one evening, after a few beers in the bar we went back to the barracks where we were staying and although I did mention if he was ok to drive he assured me he was and subsequently he started to drive and then managed to hit most of the cars on the club driveway but when we got out of the car we realised that nobody had seen or heard anything so we parked the battered car in line with the other battered cars and walked off and got a taxi.

The next day when we got back to the club we were told that someone had damaged loads of cars and unfortunately one of those car belonged to Jock, it took a lot of bottle for him to try and look upset.

Another pastime that used to happen at the club was if the weather was no good, for instance, if there was low cloud you could attach a rope to the back of a land rover and attach the other end to an open parachute, a couple of mates then throw the parachute in the air as the land rover moves off and you then take off and very soon you are very high, although that does depend on how much rope is available and you then undo the rope and parachute down for a normal landing, oh what fun.

So, what you can get an idea of is that the parachute club was a great place to hang out even if circumstances meant that you could not jump, you could still have a lot of fun.

After returning to the regiment after the course I then became the fourth member of the parashot team and we then spent the next few weeks in training and practicing for all eventuality's prior to the competition and after doing the course and all the hard work of training I ended up as the reserve so did not even get a chance to jump out of a different aircraft but I was there supporting our team who won the parachute jump trophy and came runner up in the military category.

If my memory serves me right the Daily Telegraph sponsored one of the trophy's but of course I was involved in the piss up that took place in our squadron club that evening.

Another of my volunteering duties was to volunteer to run the squadron club which at the time I thought was a good job but I did not realise that it was bloody hard work and although sometimes did not get to bed till about1am after clearing up and washing all of the glasses, I was still woke up when the rest of the lads got up for work so most of the time I was totally knackered and I then managed after a short time to get out of it by finding another volunteer.

Another job that I got which I do not think that I volunteered for was to become the Generals 3rd driver which was an interesting and varied job as I lived in the Generals house and one of my duties was to collect and drop off some of the civilian staff who worked there but as we are talking of nearly 50 years ago I have forgotten their names but there was one member of staff who lived near the centre of Bielefeld who I got on very well with and for a short time I even went out with her daughter who in the end I think that she married a friend of mine but every morning when I went to pick up the member of staff her mother, who lived with them and had a ground floor room, would hang out of her window and give me an apple or an orange which at the time, even as a young man I thought it was very nice of her but when I stopped going out with her granddaughter the fruit stopped.

The General was a really nice man and treated even the youngest staff with respect as did his lovely wife who I did also drive on one or two occasions but if England were playing football the General would come into our quarters to watch the game but he would also bring in some beers for the lads.

There was another occasion when there was some sort of fancy dress party going on at our squadron club and I cannot remember why but I know that everyone was going and they would all be in fancy dress but as the General lived a few miles away from the regiment I did not think that I could go but one of the other staff told the Generals wife and she not only arranged for the duty driver to pick me up and return me but she also helped me with my fancy dress outfit, making me a Chinese type hat and a long black moustache made from wool, I had a pair of black trouser and the Generals wife also lent me a Chinese type shirt to help with my role as a Chinaman, what a lovely lady she was.

On one occasion when there was some form of crisis down at HQ the General woke me in the middle of the night with a cup of tea and told me to get ready as he had to go to the HQ straight away, that was the time when the Russians lined up tanks on either side of the Berlin corridor just to show us how many weapons they had and the General commented that if they turned and invaded us they would be in Whitehall before we could get to Berlin.

There was so much going on at that time and I also did a fair bit of babysitting for some of my married friends which meant you did not get paid as such but they would always leave you some good food and a few beers in the fridge and it is a shame that in old age I cannot remember all of their names.

About this time we had a new man posted into our squadron from Malaya and I can't say that I liked him very much when we first met but after a short time we became very good friends and although he was single at the time he did have a girlfriend back in England who he subsequently married and she came to live in Bielefeld, my friends initials were GP and his wife was E and she was a really nice lady with a great sense of humour and even years after I left Bielefeld we stayed in touch and I stayed with them both in Germany and in England.

They lived in a flat owned by an elderly German called Jerry (yes I know and even I found that ironic) who spoke pretty good English and we would often chat to him over a couple of beers and when I asked him what he did in the war he said that he was in the Hitler Youth organisation and he also informed us that according to most German's there was only Hitler and Jerry involved as nobody else would openly own up to that and even to this day I believe that I am the only soldier to leave the army who was not in the SAS, Para's or the Marines !!

One of the nice things about being stationed there was, as mentioned earlier, a bar just outside of the back gates and when we first arrived we knew nothing about German food but we soon got the hang of it and to this day I still enjoy a good German Bratwurst or Bockwurst which are both now readily available in our local shops, another dish sold at that pub was their specialty dish called Paprika Chicken, now bear in mind that as a young person we had never heard of this thing called Paprika and we were pleasantly surprised to find that it was a fantastic dish, it was slow cooked and even the bones were edible but the only problem was that the pub only had so much room in their ovens and as the chicken was slow roasted there were only a limited amount each night so you either had to get there very early, which I am sure they preferred as you then spent more money or you chatted up the landlady the night before and she would save you one, oh the memories.

It was in the same bar one evening when it was packed and I was trying to get to the bar to order some drinks and there was this huge soldier from the regiment down the road who seemed to be blocking the way for others to get to the bar, so I was pushing my way through when he said "you have big elbows" now one of my big problems in life has always been, and still is the ability for my mouth to reply prior to my brain being in gear and on this occasion I replied "and you have a big mouth" now bearing in mind the size of this bloke it was not a sensible retort and I realised that very soon after he punched me and sent me sprawling on my arse to the other end of the pub.

Now this was not totally negative as he was thrown out of the pub and every time I then went to the bar the staff served me immediately and apart from a very sore black eye the evening ended on a positive note.

We had some very good officers and one in particular Lt G was a good bloke and I often drove him on various occasions and I think it was him that I drove to Hamelin to attend some sort of evening seminar (probably about the pied piper) and after dropping him off I went into the NAAFI to meet up unexpectedly to a very good mate of mine from training called J and he came from Kent and subsequently we had a drink and by the time I was due to pick up the officer I was half pissed, now he must have noticed this but said it had been a long day and I looked very tired (that's a new name for it) so he would drive back and in fairness to him, as far as I knew he never told anyone about that incident, what a good officer.

We also had 2 good Squadron Sergeant Majors the first one was known to us all as K and yes he was the one that got me involved in the Nijmegen marches and if I remember right I did 2 or 3 with K who knew his men and how to encourage and energise them and on one occasion on the last day of Nijmegen we were all shattered as we had already walked 150 kilometer's and still had 50 to go and by the time we had left our tent and got to the start we looked a sorry lot but K recognised this and told us all to sit down at the side of the road, now this was a bit unusual and we all wondered what he was playing at.

We then we realised that just up the road a coach was unloading a Scottish pipe band and for anyone who has marched behind a pipe band will know it has this way of motivating you and before you know it you are stood upright and are marching as though you were on the parade square and it was a great shame when they stopped after a couple of miles but of course by then we were full of enthusiasm to get to the end of the day and the end of the march and guess what, yes you are right, a few beers !!

The other Squadron Sergeant Major was a short man called SSM A who again knew his men and he enjoyed skiing at the weekend in the season down at the corps ski lodge in the Hartz mountains but if he went on his own he had to pay for his own petrol and other expenses but if he took one of his squadron then it was an activity and he could claim back all of his expenses, so a couple of times he asked me if I wanted to go with him and as it made a change from life in the barracks I was very happy to go plus he was a very nice bloke and very interesting to talk to on the journey.

In our location we had a sort of regiment of men who came from areas of the soviet union such as Latvia or Lithuania and other places that I had never heard of in those days and I cannot remember what they were called but I think it was 3 initials and although many of them were not very happy, which was probably due to their past.

Many of them spoke English as well as German and they would get involved to an extent with the rest of us but I cannot remember them drinking with us so they may have had their own bar and they always seemed to be in uniform even when off duty, which was a little strange.

One pay night myself and a few friends had gone out down town for a few drinks and a dance and on our way back to the barracks we stopped in a local bar for a few more beers and by the time we left we were all a little pissed and as we were walking back to camp an alarm went off at a local business, we did not give it a thought until someone started shouting at us so one of the lads had a great idea, run, run they shouted and we all started to run and soon after we heard a very loud bang and when we looked round there were a number of police with their weapons drawn chasing us down the road, now when you see a local copper with his handgun pointing at you it does tend to focus the mind, we were then questioned by the police and we were told that the police had been called to a burglary and when they got there they saw a group of men running away, yes, that was us but we all had the distinct feeling that while they were chasing a group of pissed soldiers the real burglar's had managed to get away and I am sure that they were very grateful to the British army for saving them from getting arrested.

There were 2 main bars that we used to go to if we had any money but if we were a bit short prior to pay day we would then of course, visit the NAAFI where the beer was very cheap.

There was also a corporals mess where the beer was even cheaper for some reason but as I had been newly promoted I did not have many friends in the mess so I would hang out with my friends and that was the place to have great laughs.

It was while I was stationed in Bielefeld that I learnt not to be put off my food by any other little incident like the occasion when a friend of mine at the next table threw up at breakfast, now this put off many people and they left their breakfast ran out of the cookhouse and they were all a little surprised when I not only finished my meal but I also ended up eating some of theirs, well it would have been a shame to waste it !!

Just down the road from our camp was what we called the bratty shop, this was the German equivalent to our fish shop and sold various fast food such as Bratwurst,

Bockwurst, chips and other things like potato salad and of course their famous and delicious mayonnaise which went magnificently with the pommes frites (chips) and even beck then in the late 60's they were great value for money and the people who ran the shop got most of their trade from the army as there were 2 regimental barracks very close to each other and I am sure that they could speak more English than they made out but at least it helped us try out our very limited German skills.

The other thing in Bielefeld that most of the younger soldiers had never seen was trams, they ran instead of buses and as you would expect from the efficient German's they were always on time and very cheap so we used them to get down and around the town.

It was while I was in Bielefeld that I had my 21st birthday which meant that I could now vote in the next general election, now bear in mind that most of the soldiers at that time had come from a very working class background and when you spoke to them about politics it became very clear that most of them felt that the Labour party represented the working classes and the Conservative party represented the middle classes and the posh such as the officers.

Now this confused me somewhat as the Labour party wanted to reduce the armed forces and close many overseas postings while the Conservatives were saying that they would keep them open and as a young soldier myself and most of my friends wanted to travel and see the world which was not going to be possible if they closed down most of the places in many parts of the world, as we all wanted to go to Hong Kong, Malaya or Singapore and many other places, so the outcome was that although it surprised many working class family's back in the UK, many young soldiers decided to vote Conservative in the hope that they would keep open as many overseas stations as possible and give us a chance to get a good posting and in many ways nothing changed in the thought process for soldiers who wanted to see the world.

In August 1969 the troubles started in Northern Ireland and from that time on many soldiers would be doing tours there and of course this carried on long after I left the army but because there was a massive amount of British army personnel in Germany at that time it did not take long before many regiments there were sending men to Northern Ireland on more than one tour and this increased over the years, bit more about that later.

Other activities at this time included watching and playing football for the squadron and one of our team, Mick P had played for Burton Albion prior to joining the army and I think he also played for the army in Germany and he was very good.

It was about this time that I was told that my mother had a heart attack and was in hospital but they knew nothing further at that time so I was told to pack up my bedding and pack a case and as soon as they had confirmation of the heart attack they would get me on the first available flight home but the problem was that my step father had been running around all day and had been at the hospital with mother so he was very tired and when asleep was very hard to wake so the police went to the house and had to bang away on the front door to get him up so that he could confirm regarding the heart attack so by the time it got back to me I had been up all night waiting.

They then got me on an RAF flight that was going back to the UK and they got it diverted to London Gatwick to deliver both myself and 4 or 5 other who were also on compassionate leave and to be honest I was very impressed with the way it was all efficiently completed including an officer waiting at Gatwick with rail warrants for us and even showed us which platform to go to for our various destinations.

Most of our work in Bielefeld was done with either land rovers or 3 ton Lorries and life was rather easy as we would often drive all over Germany on our own which did mean that we could have a sly fag while driving along but of course you had to keep an eye out in case the military police or someone else in authority saw what you were doing or if it was in the summer you could stop in a lay-by and stretch your legs and have a fag and of course, this was allowed.

Another of our roles meant that we supported a Royal Signals Regiment in all areas of transport on exercises and this sometimes meant that we would drive the vehicles with much confidential signalling equipment in the vehicle and when this happened we would go to their camp the day before the exercise was due to start to ensure that our equipment was loaded on to the correct vehicles but this then meant that we had an evening to spare but were not allowed off camp so we would all end up in the NAAFI getting pissed (yet again) but the NAAFI was at one end of the camp and our quarters were at the other end of the camp and after an evening of drinking beer it was not long before I needed to go to the toilet.

Now I could not do it on the road that ran through the camp so I went behind some huts and went for a pee up against the fence, seemed like a good idea at the time.

As I started peeing I heard a faint sort of roar and wondered what it was and at that moment there was an enormous roar and when I looked up, right in front of me was a bloody lion, so being a good soldier I just ran but unfortunately I was still in the middle of a piss, so with penis flapping in the wind (ok, ok, I may be exaggerating slightly) and urine going all over the place I made it back to our hut unharmed but everyone was asleep so I could not even tell them how brave I had been but the next morning at breakfast all the lads that were stationed at that camp rolled around laughing when they told me that there was a zoo next door and the lion was behind a very high fence with a sort of roof on top which meant it could not get out but how the bloody hell was I to know that !!!

Another job that I volunteered for was to be part of a convoy of signals trucks that had to be brought back to the UK for upgrading of the equipment and we drove down to the sea but I am not sure what port it was but there was a Navy reserve ship there which brought us and the vehicles back to the UK and about 15 years later that same ship was sunk as part of the Falklands conflict.

I think my time in Bielefeld was the turning point in my life and that was when I started to grow up and that continues to this day, although my wife may say that it has not worked very well, but I met loads of great people, made a load of friends and got a lot of help and guidance from both senior ranks and officers although on one occasion the troop commander asked me to look after his dog but I had a job to deliver something about an hour's drive away but he said it was ok as I could take the dog with me and everything went well until on the way back I stopped in a layby to let the dog go to the toilet and the bloody thing ran off and I then spent over an hour trying to catch it which, as luck would have it, I managed to do but the troop commander wanted to know why it took me so long, I told him the truth and he could not stop laughing, bastard.

I had been at Bielefeld for a couple of years and as a young soldier I wanted to move on and see the world so I started to ask some of the older soldiers how to get a decent posting somewhere interesting and where I have not been before, most of them just laughed but asked where I thought that I would like to go to, well Singapore sounds good I said and they just laughed more and even when I spoke to senior ranks they thought that I would have no chance but my mate GP suggested that instead of asking the whole bloody regiment what they thought why don't you just go to the squadron office and put in a request for a posting to Singapore and as that sounded a good idea I thought that I would give it a try even though the lads in the office thought it very unlikely they put forward my request.

A few weeks later I was working in the troop compound when a clerk came by, smiled and just said "Jammy bastard" and a short time later the troop sergeant told me I had to report to the squadron office and although he was smiling he said no more so I arrived at the office to be met by a big cheer and that was when they told me that my application for a posting to Singapore had been successful.

Wow, I had already been to Holland, Belgium, Denmark, Norway and Cyprus and now I was off to the far east but as I had amassed a fair amount of stuff over the couple of years I needed a car to take all of my stuff home to Blighty and as it happened a new bloke had been posted to us and had come by car and he now wanted to sell it as he wanted a left hand drive car so I bought his Austin Cambridge car which was a big car and would take all of my gear.

So it was with a bit of a heavy heart that I left Bielefeld to start yet another adventure but this time it was on the other side of the world but at least I had a couple of weeks leave and my cousin had also been speaking to my mum and she said that she was interested in buying my car when I was leaving for Singapore, wow a result.

I left Bielefeld late at night to avoid lots of traffic and I was going to drive through Holland and into Belgium to catch the ferry from Ostend to Dover and it was late in the night when I stopped in the middle of nowhere to have a pee and when I got back in the car, it was dead and would not start.

Now I had a couple of serious problems, the first being I had no breakdown insurance and the second was that for the past few weeks I had been sending money home so that I had enough to have a good time on leave but this led to me only having enough money for food and petrol, at this point I did not have a clue what I was going to do and out of desperation tried once more to see if it would start and bloody hell it started and believe it or not it did not do that again and I not only got home but it was ok for the whole of my leave.

Chapter Six

Off to Singapore

We flew to Singapore in an RAF aircraft but I am not sure but I think it may have been a Comet but we had to report to the RAF base the day before flying so that our bags could be searched for security reasons as Sir Alec Douglas-Home was also flying with us although most of us did not know that until we were in the air.

Do remember in those days we had to refuel twice on our journey to Singapore, the first stop was in Bahrain and when we got out of the aircraft it was very, very hot and it was only then that I started to think about the heat in Singapore and what it would be like.

Our next stop was in the Maldives on an island called Gan but to be honest I had never heard of the Maldives and only found out later that it was in the Indian ocean but when we landed they told us that there would be a delay as there was a minor fault that had to be fixed.

We were shown to a bar near the end of the runway where we were not to bothered how long the repair would take but unfortunately it did not take long at all and we were soon back in the air.

At one point during the night most of the lads were sleeping but I was still reading and Sir Alec stretched his legs and came back to our section of the plane and spoke to those who were awake for a few minutes and I found him to be a nice bloke.

When we arrived in Singapore it was very hot and also very humid and I thought that I will never get used to this, we were met by transport at Changi Airport and taken to our new posting and when we arrived there were a couple of the lads waiting for us to show us our billets and to show us where to get our bedding and waiting for me was Andy from our trade training and from Catterick who when he heard the names of the new arrivals had not only made sure he was meeting me but had already arranged to pick up my bedding and when we got to the billet the lads had already made my bed which meant we could go and get a couple of beers before bed and he then also told me that cold arse was also there but as he was in the Royal Electrical and Mechanical Engineers (REME) he was not in the same billets as us but we would meet up with him again the next day.

I also met some of the lads from the squadron but one particular soldier was a pain in the arse and in fact was a bit of a bully which I only recognised much later but as I have rather big ears he started to call me Dumbo which I must say did not bother me that much.

Most of the other lads thought it was not on but like many things in life, karma kicks in and on the flight back to the UK, where his wife and daughter were going to meet the flight, he started to have pain when he peed and very soon realised that he had a sexually transmitted disease, now that should go down a treat with his wife who I am sure was looking forward to a sexual reunion.

In those days the army seemed to be more person orientated and to that end when you arrived in a hot and humid country like Singapore they gave you a week's acclimatisation leave to enable you to get used both the heat and what was worse was the humidity which made you feel like you could not breath and you think that you will never get used to it but of course you do and after 2 or 3 weeks you rarely notice it except for the odd day or two.

As in any hot country we would start work at 07.00 but finish by about 12.30 and most of the lads would have lunch and then have a nap during the hottest part of the day but on arrival Andy told me that after he finished work the next day we would not have lunch but he would like to show me some bits around the city and so we started at a place called the Tiger Balm gardens which was a little weird as if I remember rightly, it seemed to be a lot of models of people inside cages, there were also other things to see and the young man from London (me) was duly impressed with it all.

After we had spent some time there Andy then suggested that we cross the road where there were a number of bars and get a beer and something to eat.

We got our beers and Andy asked me if I had ever has satay, "no, what is that" and he told me that it was meat on a skewer that you then dipped into a peanut sauce and although I had never tasted that, it did sound rather nice, so he ordered 12 which at that time I thought was a bit excessive until they arrived and I realised that they were only about 4 or 5 inches long with the meat cut very fine and they were delicious with the peanut sauce and after another couple of Tiger beers we again ordered that satay, now this was the life, sat outside of the bar, in the shade eating satay and drinking beer and it was only after our third lot of satay that when the man came to clear the table I asked him what meat it was because the texture was not like chicken, now the man could not speak a lot of English and we had to use signs to try to get across what we meant and then he realised what we were asking and looked around before pointing to a stray dog and he did not see this as we saw it but we managed not to throw up and after that we were told that many of the smaller bars that sold satay used dog meat but the larger bars in the city centre used chicken but I never did have another satay while I was there.

Soon after arriving I was introduced to the char whaler (the tea and rolls man) and the laundry whaler (who collected, washed, pressed and returned your laundry all in the same day) who both did great jobs and if you were not well or had a bad hangover at the week-end the char whaler would come to your billet to take your order and he then delivered it to you very soon after.

Of course, not all of the lads were that keen on tea and we did have one or two lads in the squadron who were dependent on alcohol or an alcoholic as some people may describe them and one of them was a friend of mine and he was in the same billet as me.

Every morning when he got out of bed at about 6am he would go to his locker, get out a bottle of brandy and drink about a quarter of the bottle and he would then go and have a shave, shower and teeth clean before going on parade and then driving up until he finished work at lunchtime but you could see by then that he needed a drink and the first thing he would do is go back to the billet and have another quarter bottle of brandy and then go to lunch and look sober as a judge.

At the week-ends we would often go to the Sandes Soldiers Home and yes it was the same as the one in Catterick only this one had a swimming pool which was very good and I cannot remember if it had a bar but I don't think so but there were places nearby where we would go for a few beers and then go back into the sunshine and the swimming pool.

After work we sometimes went to the local shops called The Dip where we would have a beer or two prior to going back to the camp but on a Friday we would go there to start with, then return to camp to get changed and have a shower and get out to the bar before the rain started at 4pm almost every day during the rainy season and a couple of beers later when the rain had stopped we then went off down town for the rest of the night and don't forget, although it had been raining and the humidity was a little better, it was still very warm and a lot more pleasant than the daytime.

When we went down town we would always end up in Boogie Street which was a place where transsexual men would hang out but so would some very attractive ladies and believe me there were times when you would not be able to tell one from the other, so if you were trying to chat up anyone you would be advised to do what was called the up and under test which required you to go up "her" skirt and under her knickers and if there were 2 lumps you knew it was not for you, although I would think that for some, it was for them but do remember that those were the days prior to when the politically correct brigade was formed, so all of the transsexual men were called shims (they were not a she nor a him) yes I know it sounds horrible now but remember we did not know any better and most of the "shims" were ex British soldiers who bought themselves out of the army and stayed in or gone back to Singapore to raise money for female hormone drugs to enhance their breasts or for some to even have surgery.

A couple of years later I showed my sister in law a photo of some of us with them she instantly recognised one of them who did an act at a gay pub her and her friends went to on a Sunday evening in London and to this day in Thailand they are known as "Lady Boys".

What we must remember is that homosexuality was not allowed nor tolerated in any form but I must say that the few gay soldiers that served with us were our friends and although we knew that they were gay nobody else would know and on one occasion when one of the senior ranks got wind of the soldier going off from camp on his own we all said that he was with us all evening when we knew he had gone to meet a gay friend, it was a very blinkered policy which stopped a lot of men and women who would have made great soldiers from joining up and it still took over 20 years for that attitude to change for the better and even then I am sure that there are many old soldiers who think that gay men or women should not be in the forces, which I find sad as all of the gay men that I knew were very good soldiers.

I was in the squadron office one day and the troop commander asked if I fancied navigating for him in a rally as his normal navigator was in hospital and I thought, what a nice little skive that will be and I was right as I was given a day off to learn about and practice the Tulip navigation system which, once you got the hang of it was very simple and very effective.

I went on my first rally with my boss and it was great fun and he was a very good driver bearing in mind that we were in a land rover and it was not easy to get it moving fast enough or even keeping it on the road at speed but we did finish the rally and as it was a national rally it went towards an RAC rally licence

We both enjoyed the rally and it was soon after that he asked if I would join up with him again for another bigger international rally up in the Cameron Highlands and it started and finished on the island of Penang which we loved and the night before the rally we all went out as there were 4 teams entered in the rally so we got 4 rickshaws and offered the man a bonus if we got to our destination first, now the other lads did the same and we had our own rickshaw formula one race going on but we did not stay out late as we had an early start the next morning.

The rally went rather well and we at least finished it and were well placed and at the end of the rally the prize presentation and end of rally dinner were held in a very posh hotel and the food was a very large buffet with large trays of huge prawns and as I had never seen prawns that big before I had some and enjoyed eating them but at about 3 in the morning I was throwing up and shitting at the same time and lucky for me at that time there was a MRS (medical receiving station) on the island to look after the soldiers who were stationed there at that time, it was small and had one ward of 4 beds and the boss took me there as I was by now in agony and they admitted me and gave me morphine to ease the pain.

When the other lads came to visit me I was just lying there and smiling at them which for months after they kept talking about it but I was then Casevacted (Casualty Evacuation) back to hospital in Singapore where I was only allowed to eat certain foods that I could keep down and I ended up being off work for a couple of weeks.

When the boss informed the hotel they told him that I was the only one reported to them and as far as they knew I must have eaten the one dodgy prawn but I stayed off prawns for some time after that.

Months later after that event I was asked if I would like to navigate for a professional driver from Australia in the very prestigious Malaysian 500 rally and they were showcasing the beach buggy which had only recently come on to the market and they wanted to promote the brand in the far east but the one that we used had been modified in many ways and had a Porsche engine and as it was very light it went like the wind but it was not very comfortable as the seat were fibreglass with no padding at all.

The rally start was in Kuala Lumpur (KL) and the finish was on the mainland by the causeway to Singapore and they paid for me to fly up to KL but the flight was delayed and by the time we landed they had a car waiting for me and I ended up putting on my jumpsuit in the back of the car and when we arrived at the start the driver was just about to go up the start ramp.

I jumped in the car said hi my name is Cookie and he said his name was Wayne and then we were off and as he knew the way out of KL it did give me a little time to get the paperwork sorted and the Tulip navigation papers ready for the first Jungle section.

Wayne was from a very well-known Australian car racing family and could he drive, I was in awe of his ability to throw the car around at speed but then again he said he could not believe that anyone could keep looking down at maps, charts or the like as he felt that he would be throwing up if it was him, but I had no problem and rarely looked up but on one occasion we were going very fast up a mountain road and when I looked up all I could see was a dirty great logging lorry taking up most of the road and as he was going downhill he was going pretty fast and I thought that we were going over the bloody edge of the mountain and I pulled in the muscles of my are to stop me from shitting myself but Wayne kept a very cool head, did not bat an eyelid and I swear that 2 wheels went over the edge and without making any comment or at least a swear word or two he just carried on but when we stopped for food he said he admired the way I did not panic or comment on that very close call, but at least I did not shit myself.

We did very well on that rally and when we got into Singapore I went back to camp for a couple of hours sleep before meeting up with Wayne at the end of rally presentation night at yet another rather posh local hotel and no I did not touch the prawns.

When I awoke the next morning I could barely walk as the time spent sitting on a very hard fibreglass car seat had taken its toll and for a few days I was in agony but I survived.

I was always the one that they came to if they wanted a volunteer and I rarely said no as most of the things sounded interesting or something that I had never done before and this time was no exception when they were asking for volunteers to go on a jungle survival course up in the north of Malaysia.

Our instructor was a Kiwi soldier (from New Zealand) called Sandy and he was a great bloke who I became friends with after the course and even ended up going to his sister-in-law's wedding and one or two other piss ups with him, one of which saw 2 senior ranks putting on a bit of a show by singing a song called "my brother sylvest" (he had a row of twenty medals on his chest) which I had never heard before but have many times since.

Sandy showed us many ways to survive in the jungle and told us about creatures such as snakes and monkey which to be honest was a million miles above our heads and as we had very few monkeys or snakes in South London I could understand why.

He showed us about plants that we could eat such as a root plant that when peeled and boiled tasted and looked like a potato and also we found out about plants that if you took off the end leafs, such as the fern, they tasted very similar to ordinary greens.

After that session we were then shown how to make a very comfortable bed and shelter and we had some mess tins, a small burner and a knife and fork and were then left to get on with trying to find food to cook and eat.

I could see and hear Sandy going round the lads helping some more than others when I heard his say "that smells bloody good, who is cooking that" yes you are correct it was me and I had boiled up the substitute greens and potatoes and then mixed them together, then fried them and made a very palatable bubble and squeak which he shared and liked very much but he could not believe that someone would have thought to have done that, but it was many years later that I found a book called "The Jungle is Neutral" and it went over many things that Sandy had been showing or telling us about.

We all thought that it was a great course and when we returned to our unit some of us kept in touch with Sandy as his camp was not that far from ours so we met on a fairly regular basis.

Sometime after the jungle survival course we then went on exercise to the Cameron Highlands and on one of the days we were having training in using a radio to communicate with HQ and each other and they put us into small groups but unfortunately they put me and my friends in the same group, never a good idea as we always messed around and this time was no exception and true to form we ended up getting lost in the jungle and as we did not know where we were, we could not really ask for help or directions.

I am sure that any request for help would have been met with the reply "Tango Sierra" which most of you will know means tough shit and then we would reply "Foxtrot Oscar" and you should not need me to explain what that means.

First we went one way then changed direction and then one of the lads thought that he could see a building through the trees which would mean habitation and a way of finding the way back to HQ.

We hacked our way through and when we made it we were confronted by a very smartly dressed Englishman with a smile on his face and welcoming us to his Tudor bar and restaurant, wow what a result and he took us in and treated us all to a few beers and believe me our troop commander could not work out how a group of men were sent into the jungle on exercise and came back to camp half pissed, but apparently this restaurant had been there many years and people came from many miles around to eat there, although it was mainly officers and their families as we would never be able to afford it.

Another of my driving jobs was to do delivery's to the Gurkha regiment near to us in Singapore and I got to know a Gurkha soldier who we called Gurung, it may be spelt wrong as it is an area in Nepal.

My mate Taffy and I got to know Gurung and he invited us to his family home for a party, there is a pattern here as every time we meet someone new, they invite us to a party at their house, but all I can say at the moment is that there was a huge difference in the standards of married quarters between us and the Gurkha's and they never complained in our company although they may have moaned like hell when we were not there.

Now the Gurkha's have a religious ceremony which includes about 4 days of prayers and then at the end of that period the youngest soldier in the regiment has the honour of chopping off a calves head with a ceremonial kukri and it must be done in one go and if it takes more than one go then that was seen as terrible and all sorts of tragedies would come their way but if it was done in one go then the celebrations would begin with lots of food and some rather dodgy alcohol but it was pretty obvious from when taffy and I arrived that there were no other non–Gurkha's present except for our CO who I must say was very surprised to see us two sat there in the middle of the Gurkha's being part of the celebrations and drinking god knows what, I am not sure how long it all lasted but I did have a pretty rotten headache for a couple of days and when we told Gurung he could not stop laughing as he saw us as a bit soft.

Life was good in Singapore because when you were stationed abroad in the forces you received an "overseas allowance" and although I cannot remember how much it was I do remember that it improved our standard of living, or should I say partying, significantly.

We still seemed to have our little routine and after having lunch we often went back to the billet for a nap and when we woke up we would shout very loud for the Char Waller who would then bring our tea up to us while we were still in bed.

Do remember that there were 4 or 6 of us in one billet which was very hot and humid and bear in mind we had no air con just the one fan in the middle of the ceiling and as far as I remember it only had one speed, it was either on or off but at least it made life a little bit more bearable.

Another job that I had was to go with a few other guys to a small island off of Singapore, the name of which I have totally forgotten, to help remove a lot of equipment as we were no longer required to be there, we went over by a commercial ferry and spent most of the day there and when it came to lunch time we were directed to a little café just down the road but remember that unlike Singapore, not many people spoke English so we thought that we might find it a little difficult to get across what we wanted but as we entered there were some locals eating what looked like a nice curry so we just pointed to that but it was only when we got it that we realised it was a fish head curry and as you went to eat it their little eyes just looked at you, oh well, we gave that a miss.

My next job lasted for a few weeks and had lots of different things going on.

There was a training company coming out to Malaysia for jungle warfare training and they would be based in Johor Bahru and they would be there for a number of weeks and 6 or 7 of us took our trucks to Changi airport in Singapore to get them and all of their equipment and transport them across the causeway to Johore and we would then stay with them for the whole of their stay which as far as I was concerned it sounded like a rather easy number.

When we arrived at the camp the vehicles had to be unloaded and many of the drivers did not see that as part of their job and just stayed in the cab while the training company soldiers unloaded the vehicles but to be honest both taffy and myself thought it was better to help them, it would get the job done quicker and also would show that we were part of the exercise and not watching from the perimeter.

When all the trucks had been unloaded all the drivers waited as a group to be shown where we would be sleeping and the RSM called TS came to us with the officer in charge, Major G, who said he was not very impressed with most of the group and because of the attitudes shown he said he wanted all of the drivers except for 2 to return to their unit as he only wanted drivers who were willing to partake and be part of the group, he then asked TS to show taffy and myself to our quarters and the rest had to leave straight away and return to the regiment in Singapore.

At that time the Gurkha's provided the cooks at the camp and the food was very good but we did wonder on that first day if we were going to get curry for breakfast but as it happened the cooks dished up a full English breakfast every day and it was magnificent.

Each day we would transport all of the men and their instructor to various location that had already been identified and if required they had booked the relevant area, they would then go into the jungle for a good distance to carry out their training, and we would go back to the camp or back to Singapore to collect further rations, booze or mail and any other requested equipment.

At the end of the day we would meet them at a pre-arranged spot to transport them all back to camp and apparently when they had finished their tasks for the day they were each given a map reference of where the trucks would be and asked to put cash in the kitty and the first person back to the transport won the money in the kitty, now I am not sure if there was some sort of fiddle going on but every time they did this the RSM, TS would win and when you considered that he was a very large man it did ensure that he got the respect of everyone.

There was not very much separation except all of the instructors slept in one area and all of the trainees slept separately and the 2 drivers also had a separate area but we all shared the same toilets and showers.

There was a staff sergeant L who had seen active service in Malaysia many years before and had been shot many times but he survived and his body was covered in scars, how on earth anyone could survive being shot so many times.

There was also another decent bloke who I will call CC and his specialty was blowing things up and would spend a fair bit of time playing with explosives, oh what fun we had with everyone scared to lift a toilet seat in case it exploded.

I must admit that we were treated very well by both the senior rank instructors and Major G and in the evening after a great meal we would all sit around and have a few beers and talk and both taffy and myself seemed to get on with all of the instructors even though they would sometimes play little tricks on us which I will not go into detail about.

On one occasion I was filling up with petrol at a local petrol station but as I left I hit an upright station which collapsed and most of the bloody roof also collapsed, now I thought that this would get me into a lot of trouble and I had to make out a rather in depth acci9dent report and the Major went and saw the owner of the garage and although they all took the piss out of me for the next couple of weeks I heard nothing else and the Gurkha's very kindly repaired my truck so even after we went back to the unit nobody knew or found out about the accident, well done Major G.

When we went back to Singapore to get supplies or mail we would go to our unit to pick our own mail or to find out if anything was going on and it was on one of those occasions that we found out that the base was closing down and most of the men would be going back to the UK.

A very small contingent would be part of the Australian, New Zealand and UK group (ANZUK) that would stay and although I immediately put in to stay as part of that group I was turned down and like the rest had to wait a few weeks to find out when we were going back and where we were being posted to.

So on my return to the camp in Johor and told them all that we were not going to be in Singapore for a lot longer they then stated asking where we thought we would like to be posted and spent a happy couple of hours fantasising of where that would be.

I loved taking any of the lads to the MRS (medical receiving station) and we would have to wait for them and you could hear all the stuff going on in the clinic cubicles and then see a soldier emerge with a great big grin on his face and I would think that he has been told it is not a sexually transmitted disease (STD) or he had one and he had just received the all clear and he was now free to go back to the brothel where he got it in the first place!!

While I was on my detachment with the training company in Johore I did get a few days of to go on yet another rally and I was getting to be known as a half decent navigator and got to the stage where I qualified for an International Rally License which I was rather proud of and in fact I went on to further rallying at my next posting.

Our time in Johore was coming to an end which both taffy and myself were rather sad about as we had started to form some friendships and had got on very well with both the trainees and the instructors and it was decided that we would hold a leaving party 2 days before they were due to fly back to the UK as the RSM felt that if we had the party on the last night none of us would be very capable the next morning and the drivers would still be drunk.

On the night of the party we had 3 large cooking vessels in the middle of the dining area, one contained rice, one was more like a casserole and the third was a spiced curry which was fantastic and all three were sat on little burners that kept the food warm for most of the night, we also had loads of crates of beer again, in the middle of the dining area.

Now this particular regiment was very proud of its drinking abilities and they thought that the two young drivers from the RCT would not be able to keep up with them but oh how wrong can you be and one by one they fell by the wayside but I must say that the RSM looked like he could have gone all week without getting totally shitfaced.

As daylight approached there was only 4 of us left, the RSM, CC, Taffy and myself and we also helped to clear up some of the mess otherwise it was down to the Gurkha's to clear up and we all felt that this was unfair.

We spent most of the last day helping to pack up all of their equipment and load it on to ours and the other trucks that had been sent to help us transport all of the gear to Changi airport the following morning and funny as this may seem, we did not feel like having a lot to drink that evening and I think it was at this point that every time we saw an aircraft somebody would wisecrack oh look there is a GHM, remember we used that term in Cyprus but see the explanation in the section on words and sayings.

The next morning we trundled off to Singapore where we unloaded the trucks and said our goodbyes although I was a little puzzled when we all shook hands and Major G said bye for now and we hope to see you soon, that sounded a bit weird but I soon forgot about it and got on with life back at our camp in Singapore.

When we were told that we would be going back to the UK I wrote to my mother to tell her and when she replied she asked if I could get some Chinese material so that she could make the 2 little girls who lived next door a Chinese dress each as it would be very different and I am not sure if she actually did finish them before she passed away but the challenge was to get this material as cheaply as possible and the place to do that was the night market.

A couple of us went to the night market as we were all looking for presents to take home and the saga of the material started, I saw some good material on a stall and told him how much I wanted and he then told me the price, now this is the point that I start laughing and then asked him for his best price, he then came down in price and I offered about half that, he then said no so I then walked away and went to another stall and when I started to haggle who appeared but the man from the last stall holding his material and he was then arguing with the other stall holder, by this time we were laughing and walked away to be followed by both men, both lowering their prices and both shouting at each other, so we found a bar and stayed out of the way for a while and when we went back to the market a young lady showed me some even nicer material at a lot lower price so I bought it from her !!

As I said earlier we had a place near to our camp that we all called the dip, this place was not huge but had some shops and a couple of bars so we would often go there after work for a beer before going back to the billet and over time we got to know the owners or workers in the various establishments and whatever we wanted to buy seemed to come down in price every time we visited so we all decided to wait until the last few days we were there before buying some of our presents to get them at a good price and I had my eye on an Omega watch which was a very good quality watch which cost a lot more back in Blighty and very slowly I ground him down to a very good price and I was very proud of that watch but when I got home on leave I saw the price of them so I sold it to buy a car.

Which just goes to show what a bargain it was and if I had known how much they were worth back home I would have bought a couple more to sell.

The other thing that I bought to take home was a "Laughing Bag" which had a small box inside the bag with a button and when you pushed the button it would give out a very long and infectious laugh, a bit like the laughing policeman and my mother loved it and remember they were hardly ever seen in the UK at that time so it was a rare novelty and of course just showed my immaturity!!

Just before we left Singapore we were all given our new posting and I was a bit surprised that I got a posting to Ashford in Kent to a regimental Depot and to be honest I would rather be overseas and not stationed in the UK but I would have to wait and see what it was like.

The flight home was a lot better than the flight out to Singapore as we only had one fuel stop and that was in Cyprus and if I remember correctly, it took very little time so we were back on the flight before we were able to even get a beer.

After our time in Singapore we were given 2 weeks leave prior to joining our new regiments and in that time we had a chance to see friends and family who we had not seen for some time and very close to my mother's house was a British Legion club which I was allowed into because I was a serving soldier.

This was a great club in Lancing in Sussex and they always welcomed me with open arms and it was in this club where I met a Welshman who had taught me to play the spoons and when I left for Singapore he gave me a present of 2 heavy silver spoons which all seemed a bit ironic as we always seemed to associate the spoons with the old East End pearly Kings and Queens and me, a Londoner was being taught to play the spoons by a Welshman.

Chapter Seven

Life in the UK

Oh dear, oh dear, posted back to England to a place that I thought would be totally boring, no overseas allowance and nobody that I would know as I was attached to a training regiment in Kent with a very small MT (motor transport) section consisting of one senior rank, one corporal, one lance corporal and a private soldier all of whom were married except me, so I was the only one living in the barracks and all of the other guys were new recruits on their training, so this did not look at all good.

The civilian drivers were all older men but they were a good laugh and they did most of the mundane work with the soldiers doing some of the interesting stuff and as part of the regiment there was a joint service wing that went all over Europe and as the married men were not keen I always volunteered and that was always interesting and fun.

I had only been there a few weeks when one Saturday I was told to report to the guardroom, when I got there they told me there was a phone call for me and when I answered it was a man from the Ministry of Defence who asked me my name, rank and number and then said "I am sorry to inform you but your mother is dead" he then went on to tell me that I could take immediate compassionate leave and I went home that afternoon and when I arrived I found my step-father was totally devastated and we sat looking at each other for some time, I offered to cook something but neither of us were hungry, now bear in mind that I was a soldier who's answer to anything where death was involved, was to go and get pissed and I suggested this to my step-father but he declined but he did give me a front door key as he thought that he would not be up when I returned.

I went to the British Legion club and was joined very soon after by 2 of my brothers and a close family friend and we all got totally shit faced and on our return home my step-father stayed in his bedroom while the rest of us carried on drinking and one had his head in the dustbin throwing up.

The next day we all decided that it would be for the best if we all left and that way my step-father would have to get himself going and make all of the relevant arrangements, so it was with a huge amount of surprise that I reported for work on the Monday as they all expected me to be on leave for a couple of weeks.

I did drive home the night before the funeral and was a little surprised that there was an open coffin with my mother laying there, because in those days many people would want to see the body and say their farewells, but not me, I wanted to remember my mother the way she was and not as a dead body.

My mother was buried and as she was rather proud that I was doing ok in the army I decided to wear my uniform but after the coffin was lowered into the grave I decided to salute at the edge of the grave (you think you know what is coming next) now as the edge of the grave was a little damp and slippy, I started to lose my footing and slid towards the grave but luckily for me my eldest brother was next to me and managed to grab hold of me, perish the thought if I had ended up in the grave, I would have never lived it down and my family would be taking the piss to this day.

After the funeral we all went back to our house where a neighbour had prepared food and drinks but I did not drink as my uncle and aunt and family were on holiday in Dymchurch in Kent at the time so as I was returning to Kent I offered them a lift, now this seemed like a good idea at the time but when we arrived at their caravans the first thing that my uncle suggested was that we all went down the pub and we all got a little drunk but the funniest part was one of my cousins had an Italian husband who could not speak a lot of English and it was bloody hilarious watching and listening to my uncle trying to tell him that it was his round, he just started getting louder with lots of hand gestures but it did work and he got in his round.

It was only a short time later when I went on my first exercise with the Joint Service Wing to Belgium and I drove the Colonel which was a cushy number as when we arrived and helped to unload equipment we then had very little to do for a few days although we had to stay on site in case we were needed for anything.

We did all of our own cooking and we would take it in turns to shop and then cook the main meal of the day and when it was my turn I bought some lovely looking steak, by using hand gestures as the local butcher did not speak English and served this up with homemade chips which they all enjoyed but the next day when the person doing the shopping returned they informed us that I had in fact bought horse meat the day before but once we all got over our initial shock we all agreed that it was in fact very good and very tasty.

When the exercise had finished we all headed back but as I was driving the colonel and a major that he offered a lift to, we left before the rest to get the earlier ferry from

Zeebruger to Dover but when we got to the port there was a huge gale and the waves were coming over the roofs of the dockside warehouses, wow I thought, this is going to be a great trip and they told us when we got on board that that would be sailing close to the coast for most of the way and then make a dash for Dover which sounded good.

We had not been on board long and we were just leaving the port when the colonel thought that it may be a good idea to have lunch early while we were hugging the coast and so we went to eat but as soon as our food came to our table the good major started to go green and rushed from the table to the toilets.

He was gone so long that the colonel and I had finished our food when he returned and as he did not want to eat we all went and sat in the lounge which was very good but when the colonel got out a very large bar of chocolate and offered it to us, the major, again, flew to the toilet and by the time he came back we were nearly at Dover, although I did spend some time helping people down the stairs to the toilets including children and the elderly and by the time we got back to our camp the major was starting to get back to a normal colour.

Do remember that all of these anecdotes are true but are not always in the correct order and I have to write them as I remember them.

We often went on lots of exercises to many parts of the country and one of the places we used to visit was at the top of a very steep hill on the edge of Plymouth and it was one hell of a desolate place and there was nowhere that you could go as any life was miles away at the bottom of the bloody hill and when people say "did you enjoy Plymouth" I can only answer I don't know as I never had the chance to go into town on those occasions.

I know that everyone takes the micky out of NAAFI meat pies and so they should but if you have been sat there for a couple of hours on the piss and you have started to feel peckish then a meat pie is all you desire or need and like on other occasions I was tempted by the NAAFI meat pie and the consequences took me back to a Penang hotel and the dreaded food poisoning.

I was taken very ill with liquid coming out of both ends and yes it was as bad as it sounds so I was sent to the MRS at Folkestone which was pretty large for an MRS, remember they were not hospitals but this one had at least 2 large wards but they also covered a regiment of boy soldiers but they were not allowed to sleep in the same ward as the men, so we ended up having one person in each ward and for some rather peculiar and unreasonable reason they put me at the far end of the ward which was the furthest from the toilet and bearing in mind what I said earlier this was not one of their best ideas and they soon realised this when there was sick and shit all the way down the ward, it was at this point that someone thought it would be a good idea if they put my bed next to the toilet and thankfully this worked a lot better and thankfully I was only there for about 4 days when they discharged me back to my unit.

The next big exercise that we did was for troops from both the UK and other EU forces and this took place in Denmark, a place I liked ever since we went through it on the train when I attended the Army Outward Bound course in Norway a few years earlier. I was the first to volunteer only this time I would be driving a 3 ton truck full of equipment and not a staff car for the colonel as on the last jaunt, we drove from Kent to

Harwich and some of the trucks also had men travelling in the back as well and we went to Esbjerg and then drove further north to where the exercise was going to take place, next to a lake and in the middle of nowhere.

After unloading the trucks myself and 4 others were shown to our sleeping quarters, wow, it was a holiday type bungalow with separate bedrooms and it was on the shore of a massive beautiful lake and the Danish air force had also allocated a liaison officer to ensure we had everything we need and he was a smashing bloke who showed us how he would go to the end of his garden, which was also on the lake and "Tickle Trout" now for a boy from South London this did sound a bit weird but when he showed us what he did I was full of admiration for both him and his dog because when he flipped the trout on to the grass the fish would try to get back in the water but his dog would go over and put a paw on the fish to keep it from getting back to the water.

Now most evenings he would supply us with fresh trout and he would also bring over his small smoking box so that we could all have a little smoked trout for our supper and as he did that for us, we would supply him with whisky which even at that time was very expensive in Denmark but we had our own duty free truck with us so it cost us very little to supply him with duty free whisky.

Of course, most of the lads bought some duty free spirits to take home although officially we were only allowed one litre each, although some of our lads took a chance and bought 2.

As a young lad we were involved in all sorts of local scams that would result in either free food, free logs or free coal but the one thing we did not do was go fishing so I was a little sceptical when our liaison officer offered to lend us fishing equipment so that we could go fishing in the lake and as we had nothing better to do we thought that we would give it a go and one of the lads had done some fishing so he became a sort of instructor and showed us how to set up the gear.

Now as I am sure you can imagine a few soldiers fishing in a lake on a rather hot summers day in Denmark did not produce the results that we had hoped for and after a few hours of getting absolutely nowhere we gave up and went for a walk around the lake and did not bother fishing again.

The exercise area where we were was very close to the Danish air force base and 2 or 3 times a week they had supplies flown up to them from Copenhagen and this was known as the "Milk run" and after a few days we were getting a little bored and usually when this happened we would volunteer to help with other non-skilled work but on this occasion we were again shocked when the liaison officer asked us if we would like to spend a couple of days in Copenhagen and he would arrange for us to sleep in the air base there which was very close to the centre of the city.

When we got to the local air base we saw what can only be described as an old war plane and if I remember correctly it was an old twin prop DC3 but the interior was very comfortable with some nice large seats and once aboard it did not take long to get to "Wonderful, Wonderful Copenhagen" and we were soon let loose on the city.

We packed a lot into a couple of days including the rather fantastic Tivoli Gardens, although, as this was about 47 years ago, I am sure that it has now changed considerably and of course bear in mind that our expectations were a lot less than the children today.

We really loved our couple of days in Copenhagen and the shame is that I have never been back since and we could not stay any longer as others wanted to book a seat on the Milk run to see the city.

On our return to our "Holiday home" we only had a few more days to go and we had to organise the loading of all the equipment and it was very kind of some of the lads who were not from our regiment, to offer to load a couple of the trucks for us which gave us a little bit more time in the sun.

There were many soldiers from different regiments on that exercise so when we arrived at Harwich on our return we had to wait for everyone to get off the boat so that we could all go our separate ways.

We went for a coffee and said our goodbyes and when I returned to my truck there were a few lads next to it and they gave me a couple of bottles of spirits and when I asked why I was told that the little dears had hidden both bottles of spirits and loads of pornographic magazines, which were freely available in Denmark, in the underside of my truck, bastards!!

I was starting to get used to life in Kent and I became very friendly with the owners of a local pub in the High Street and when I visited the town some months later I stayed with them as they did bed and breakfast but they very kindly did not charge me at all, well, only for the beer that I drank in the evenings and of course I got to know lots of local people and local girls and I met a lovely girl and our relationship became very serious and after a few months we became engaged but more of that later.

At about this time the IRA were blowing up anything to do with the British army including trying to blow up barracks in Germany, so security was very strict and everyone was ordered to be very diligent so when I went over to HQ to collect mail I was very surprised to hear the general alarm go off just as I entered the building, Out, Out shouted the sergeant major and as I looked up the stair there was a very frightened looking recruit holding a package at arm's length coming towards the exit, well I could not help it as I started laughing "what are you laughing at" shouted the sergeant major, and I replied that if the bloody thing exploded he would be dead anyway, so why not just stick it under your arm and walk out.

Ok said the sergeant major you bloody carry it out to the middle of the playing field and so I did and yes I was still laughing and I had to laugh even more when the bomb disposal team used a controlled explosion to blow up what turned out to be a book ordered by the Commanding Officer who was not there that morning and I am sure he was not at all happy although he did say it was better to be safe than sorry.

I did enjoy my football and still played when I went to Kent and was picked for the training regimental team which I enjoyed as we played other regiments from Kent, Surrey, Sussex and London but on one occasion when we were playing at home I was approached by an officer who had been watching the football game and he asked me if I would like to join the regimental rugby team, now anyone else this may have hurt their feelings but I was chuffed that he saw potential for rugby whilst playing football.

As I was also into motor sport I started to organise various motor activity events within the camp for the recruits, permanent staff and their families and included such thing as trying to reverse a trailer, a speed section where you had to go in and out of bollards at speed and various other silly motoring games, which I must say were enjoyed by almost everyone including things for younger children.

I then started to organise a rally team to compete in civilian rally's all over the place and as we had a few Mini's in the transport section they proved to be ideal and all I then needed were drivers and of course, navigators who I had to train and that was also great fun as most of them had never been driven at speed before.

My eldest brother was a self-taught motor mechanic and he lived in South London which was very helpful as he used to pep up the engines a bit or knock out the bumps that we had done on the rally and we could stop off to him on the way back to

Kent from places like Anglesey in North Wales where there are some great rally stages along some very narrow and winding tracks and on one occasion I was going much to fast on the approach to a bridge and if fact bounced all along the wall of the bridge and the back-up team were waiting as they knew what would happen, to pull out the bodywork that was resting on the tyres and even my brother could not help me then and my boss was not very happy when I took back a rather battered car.

We had a really nice NAAFI manageress who used to listed to all of the recruits problems and who was like a substitute mother to most of those young lads who would come into the NAAFI to tell her either their very good news or to seek sympathy on their bad news and I got on with her so well that she lent me some money so that I could buy a car.

During my time in Kent I owned 3 different cars, a Ford Prefect, an Austin A35 and a Ford Anglia which were all good cars in their own way for instance when my nephew got married I decided that the grey paintwork on my A35 was a bit faded and made the car look knackered, which it was not, so I decided that it needed a re-spray but as I could not afford that the only other way was for me to do it myself, no, not with a spray gun but with a paintbrush, oh dear I hear you say but actually it turned out ok and the car looked so much cleaner and neater and you only saw the brush marks if you looked very closely but I had no trouble selling it.

While I was stationed in Kent I did go up to Salford on a couple of occasions and stayed with JG and his wife who were friends of Tich, my mate from training and Catterick and as I was single with no parents now alive I could go away for week-ends whenever I liked and my mate GP and his wife E who were still stationed in Bielefeld were on leave and invited me down to Bournmouth for the week-end which I think was for the christening of their daughter and I was one of the god parents which I loved.

During that time in Bournmouth I met a really nice girl who lived on her own with her little boy who was only a toddler at the time and although I went and stayed with her on one occasion it was not going to last so we both decided that we would go no further.

Back in Kent I met a lovely local girl as I said earlier and the relationship soon blossomed and yes it looked like this was it and we decided to get married but as time went on I was getting cold feet and the question I kept asking myself was could I spend the rest of my life with this young lady, bearing in mind I was only 24 but if I just broke off the relationship her family and friends would kill me, but then I had a dastardly plan so I applied for a posting back to Germany which I had enjoyed so much before but at this point I did not mention this to my fiancé and it very soon came through that I was to be stationed in Munster in Germany, now being one of life's cowards I was not sure how to tell my fiancé that 1) I was being posted to Germany and 2) the wedding was off and as the wedding was only 6 weeks away and people had bought new suits and dresses and various other expenses I asked my colleagues what to do, I just wanted to run but they all said that was not fair on the young lady and that I should tell her, which I did, by phone a few days before I was due to leave and for the next few days she was phoning and coming to the camp to try and find me but the problem that I had was that although she was a smashing young lady I was not ready or mature enough to be a husband and so like all brave soldiers I hid until it was the day I left and yes I did feel terrible and I am sure that she was devastated and so was I.

But sometimes things in life do catch up with you and after making friends with a smashing couple who when I told them about leaving the UK in a hurry informed me that everyone feels like I felt just prior to their wedding and my feelings about spending the rest of my life with that young lady were normal pre-wedding nerves. All of a sudden I thought that I had already made a massive mistake in my life but there was nothing I could do about it or so I thought but my friends persuaded me otherwise and suggested that I ask for a few days off and as I still had my trusted car, drive back to England and tell her that the wedding is back on but a little delayed.

I asked for and got 5 days leave and with the 2 week-ends that made 9 days and I felt that would be enough time to put the record straight and arrange another date for the wedding, so I drove all the way back to England, booked a few nights B & B in my friends pub and contacted my former fiancé.

Now this may come as a surprise to you as indeed it did to me but in a rather un-ladylike manner she told me to F*** off and that she never wanted to see or to hear from me ever again and unless I left her alone she would ask her family to sort me out, now I am the sort of bloke that can take a hint and so I cut my visit short and drove back to Germany, so that's what they call karma!!

I was now in a place called Munster in Germany and as normal I made friends very quickly with both the single lads and the married men and soon started babysitting again which I liked as it got you out of the camp for a few hours and they always left you a few beers and some food but remember we did not have microwaves way back then and if they had made you something like a shepherd's pie you would have to heat it up again in the oven and of course that could take ages.

Often I was offered to stay the night and one particular friend had a young little boy and he slept in one bed and I slept in another bed in the same room and as you are aware young children wake up early and he took great pleasure In taking off his nappy and coming over to me and would sit on my head which I must say I found this a little concerning but when I told his parents about it they just burst out laughing and said that he does that to anyone staying and even though they have told him that this is not very nice he continued to do it but to be fair although I would sometimes go back to camp smelling of piss I was very lucky and never went back smelling of shit!!

I was still taking part in most sports and I also did a couple more Nijmegen marches which were great fun most of the time and even more so when you had time to train properly and that would keep the blisters to a minimum.

We also had a regimental 5 a side football competition and as the assistant manager for the squadron football team I was asked to pick some teams from our normal squad and if there were any others then make up more teams which I did but there were still a few blokes who would want to take part including PB a young lad who had just been posted to us, so I decided to make up another team but as they had no goalkeeper I said that for a laugh I would step in but what we did not know was that the young newly arrived lad was a very, very good footballer named PB who became a very good friend of mine and much to the surprise of everyone, including me, we managed to win the bloody competition.

I was the assistant manager to the squadron football team and the manager was the squadron quartermaster, a staff sergeant (known to us as H) who asked me if I would like to work for him in the stores and although at first you may think that I would find this boring, you would be wrong because this job had so many positive things going for it, for a start I got my own rather large room down in the stores which meant that I did not get inspected like the other guys and going on exercise was almost a pleasure also down in another part of the cellar was the squadron club which was the centre of most good nights and I might add, early mornings and it has been known for us to get one of the lads to go over to the cookhouse as soon as breakfast started to bring us all back bacon sarnies so that we could carry on drinking but being nice fair minded guys we would also help the barman clear up ready for the Saturday or Sunday opening times, yes we only did that at the week-ends and of course it was not always the junior ranks who were on the piss as above the entrance door there was a sign that said "abandon rank all ye who enter" so sometimes there was a senior rank who just wanted to get away from the sergeants mess.

When we went on exercise he would make sure that we had all the equipment that we needed but in my case he made sure that in the back of the truck was a bed with mattress, a blanket which was hung up a became a curtain and of course in the winter he would make sure that I also had a paraffin stove to keep warm but the stove also acted as a cooking stove if you took the top lid off and put a saucepan on top you could cook most things.

I would often cook a nice curry but as the officers went pass and smelt the curry they would make some sort of excuse to climb in the back of the truck and manage to get some curry.

Now, unfortunately this created a precedence and when we went on other exercises some of the officers would call round to see what was cooking and some even brought some fresh meat or fresh veg which made life so much more pleasant.

I had a young mate who lived near Dorking in Surrey who I will call J and he offered to put me up when we were on leave and his mum was a lovely lady and he also had an older brother and sister and I cannot remember how but J had a very small Fiat car that was overheating and was generally knackered but when we looked at it we decided that there was a leak in the head gasket and we decided that we would replace it, bearing in mind that the car engines in those days (in a 60's car) were very simple, they did not require a computer to tell you what the fault was, you could nearly always see the problem, now as it happened J and I managed to replace a head gasket and we used the car for the rest of our leave which included a trip to see his sister who lived in Reading which was where I got on a horse for the first time in my life and as I was from London and not a country boy this could only end in one way and when the rest started to trot I was just hanging on for dear life so did not see the branch of the tree overhanging the path, yes, ok, easy for you to work out, but as I was laying on the path it did at least give the others a very good laugh.

Soon after that our leave was over and for the life of me I cannot remember what happened to that car as I am sure that we flew back to Germany and returned to Munster.

Another good thing about that job was that H the quartermaster thought that I deserved promotion and put me forward for it so that meant that I got an increase in pay which was a good thing, I really enjoyed working for H but around this time his daughter became very ill with, if I remember right, was some form of cancer and she was referred to hospital in London and as he and his wife had other children it was going to be very difficult for him and in situations like this the army are very good and not only gave him a posting to London (Woolwich) but also gave him promotion, more about him and his family later.

We worked very closely with an American army unit that was near to us and we often went on exercises with them and their compo rations were far better than ours and they even had cigarettes as part of their compo rations which did cause some concern when I asked an American soldier if he wanted "a fag" which to me meant a cigarette but of course to him it meant a gay person and his little face was a picture until one of his mates told him what I meant.

Another great thing about the regiment was that we went on a summer camp each year and I have forgotten where we went but it was to a tented camp up in the hills and miles from anywhere but we had loads of fun including 5 a side football and bearing in mind my last 5 a side competition I was asked to go in goal and played pretty well but do remember that a 5 a side goal is much smaller than a full size goal but on our return I was asked to play in goal for the squadron side but although I did not let in any goals, I did not play in goal again, which was probably for the best.

Another activity was what we called a death slide or a Zip Wire as it is now known in civvy street and although I was not part of the team that put it up I was very impressed as it was a huge slide that went down the hill and across a dip to the next hill and when they had finished doing it I offered to do the test run but the senior rank who was in charge refused my offer and said that he had to do it, but now we come to the tragic bit, he went off ok but about half way down and at its highest point the whole bloody thing collapsed and he fell from a great height to the ground and was severely injured and I believe that he ended up with a very bad disability and was medically discharged and even now I shudder to think that it could have been me,

I was still volunteering for all or any activity which got me out of soldiering and that included both PB and myself going with the Officer Commanding (OC) on a sailing course to the Dummersee, which was a very large man-made lake where our corps had a sailing school but it was also used by many other regiments.

While we were on the course there was a competition between the RCT and another corps and one of our officers Captain H was a very good sailor and represented the army in Germany and he had a soldier who crewed for him but on this occasion for some reason he did not turn up so Captain H asked the instructor if he could borrow someone from the course and yes, you are right, it was me but only after a couple of others made excuses as the weather was terrible, cold, wet and windy.

We went out to the start of the race a little early to try and get to know how we would work and it seemed ok, so we headed to the start line and just before the gun went off we managed to capsize, but as I had been taught capsize drill the day before I did know what I was supposed to do but it is rather off putting when trying to right the boat, the bloody start gun went off and the rest of them were off and away, oh well so what if we come last but as it happened the weather was so bad that most of the others either capsized or made other mistakes and we just kept laughing and in fact we managed to get second place and we won a runners up trophy which was not bad as I was still on the course, but the good thing was that Captain H wanted me as his crew and we went on to win a couple more trophies but I must add that it was in the main due to his sailing skills and ability rather than anything that I could contribute but we made sure we always had fun although there were times when he called me a few unsavoury names during races.

As PB was a very good all round sportsman he was our representative in a tennis competition a few weeks away but he needed to do a lot of training and tennis practice to get in the best possible shape so he asked the OC if I could be a training partner for him as he needed someone to get the balls back to him and as I was not very good at tennis but ok as a ball boy the OC said yes and it was yet again a very nice little job, which I had the habit of getting or being in the right place at the right time.

Sometimes when I went on leave from Germany I would stay at the Union Jack Club in London and PB's mum and dad looked after a very large house for a well off American man and they lived in the house in one of the most expensive squares in the capital so PB and I would meet up to either go to a football match or to have a kick around in Hyde Park which just made my leave a little bit nicer.

About this time I was going to the yacht club a lot and so was the OC and on one occasion he found out that the sergeant running the club had done his time there and was being returned to his unit and they were looking for a new manager so on his return to the camp he called me to his office and asked me if I would like to be promoted to sergeant and to run the yacht club which would mean living up at the club all summer in a caravan and then going to another regiment in the winter to repair and renovate the boats ready for the next season and to be honest this sounded great to me and so I got promotion and a cushy little number at the yacht club and as it was summer it was great.

We ran courses for armed services personnel during the week and at weekends we ran courses for children and we also had families come for a day or even the week-end as we did have a few rooms and most of the families were either officers or senior ranks but most of them were really nice although we did have the odd dickhead who felt that because they were officers they should get preferential treatment by all of the staff.

One of the officers wives would come with him and their son and when they went sailing she would stay in the yacht club and talk to other wives, read or chat with the staff and she suggested that I would get on a lot better if I had elocution lessons which made me smile, although I was aware of how common I sounded and although I sound a lot better now, I still sound common which is ok by me.

Very close to the yacht club were a few shops, a bar and a restaurant which I occasionally visited just to get a change of scenery every now and again and if any of the lads came up from my regiment we would go there just to get away from the hustle and bustle of the club.

And I do remember when the OC, PB and myself were on our sailing course we decided to eat out in that restaurant on one occasion and the OC did not know what to say when, at the end of the meal, we said that it would be dead easy to do a runner and not pay the bill.

He thought for a moment that we meant it and it was only when we both burst out laughing that he realised that it was in fact a joke aimed at winding him up, which of course, it did.

Like every good summer it had to come to an end and after all of the courses had finished most of the men went back to their regiments but the boatman and me went to the nearest regiment with all of the boats to get them ready for the next spring when the yacht club would re-open.

I was put up in the sergeants mess which was not a bad place and I had another sergeant show me around, introduced me to other members of the mess and asked me, more in hope than anything else, if I played football as they had the second leg of a cup match due, they were 3-0 down in the first leg and could do with some help and although I pointed out that I was not that good they did realise that I was a lot younger than most of them so at least I would be able to run faster than most of the opposition and we did very well and won the game 4-0 and got into the next round and if I remember rightly I scored a goal or two but as I was quicker than them I also managed to assist in two of the goals so I came out of it as a bit of a hero.

Apart from the football life became boring and predictable with every day just repairing and renovating our boats and in most cases this meant using paint remover to get all of the muck and old paint off and then re-painting the whole boat and it was on one of those occasions that I got paint stripper splash into my eye and that meant that I could not drive and was out of action for a short while.

After my eye got better I used the week-ends to either go back to my regiment in Munster or visit my good friends GP and E and their daughter in Bielefeld which I enjoyed very much.

But as the winter went on my daily grind was getting the better of me and as I had met a local girl, (yes I know, another local girl) we decided to go away for the week-end but then stayed at a country hotel for a little longer which then meant that I was absent without leave (AWOL) and on my return I was demoted, left the other guy doing all the work on the boats and brought back to the regiment and moved to another squadron within the regiment.

Chapter Eight

Germany and beyond

Before I start going on about Northern Ireland I will say that my father was Irish and born in Dublin and although a lot of his history is a bit hazy he used to sing the Irish rebel songs all the time and when he was pissed you could often hear him coming down the road singing "Kevin Barry" and of course as a child you learn the words but do not know the meaning or the reason behind the song. A tour of Northern Ireland normally lasted for 4 months, you worked all day every day and at times when the troubles were at their height you would also work at night if that was needed but you were allowed 4 days R & R (rest and recuperation) or if you were married you might have called it romp and resuscitation and some went back to their regiments which could have been in England or in Germany.

Before going on a tour of Northern Ireland you had a period of training with the troops they you were going with and it did not matter if you had been before, some soldiers have done 4 or 5 tours but you still had to do the pre-tour training and this included physical training as well and on one occasion they decided that with just about a week to go before deployment we were all pretty fit so we could have a game of murder ball, now for those of you who may not be familiar with this game the rules are pretty simple, all of the men are split into 2 groups, one group takes off their tops so now we have 2 distinct teams and in the middle is placed a medicine ball (a large very heavy ball used for gym work) and by hook or by crook you had to get the ball to the opposite end of the hall.

Somehow during this rather unsightly fracas I managed to get seriously hurt and tore all of the muscles in my shoulder which meant I could not lift my arm very high and as there was a need in Northern Ireland to carry and if needed, use a rifle then I would have been up shit street and the doctor was going to say I was unfit for the tour but I managed to persuade him that at least for the first week or so I did not need to leave our location and by that time it would have healed and so he agreed to let me go.

So off to Belfast I went with my right arm strapped up and carrying my rifle in my left hand and if we had run into any trouble when we first arrived I would have been knackered as there was no way that I could have fired an SLR accurately with my left hand, it was hard enough to be accurate with my right hand !!

For the younger soldiers, being there could be very frightening and intimidating which meant the older soldiers had to be the calming influence and of course there were also some very funny things that happened and many of those incidents may have happened to many soldiers over the years.

Driving down the Springfield Road one day a member of the public waved us down to tell us that there was a package outside of a protestant pub, we pulled across the road to stop the traffic and I deployed one soldier each end of the road block for safety reasons and I then told one of the lads to have a look at the package and as per the training his job was to just ensure it was not an empty box (which was done a lot just to cause disruption) and if he thought it was not an empty box I would then have to decide to call in bomb disposal but bear in mind that this would cause total disruption to the whole area, the lad in question was a little worried but he then went up to the box and stamped all over and then came back to me to declare that the box was empty, I will not disclose his name nor my reply but the other lads, who were well away had it exploded, found it bloody hilarious.

The living conditions for soldiers in most area of Northern Ireland were appalling with places such as police stations or old mills used as accommodation with as many as about 12 or 14 men to one room and of course no privacy at all and if you all tried to get up at once if the general alarm went off then it was very tight.

In Belfast most of the accommodation was either in or near the Springfield Road or the Falls road and both areas could be seen as volatile but in a lot of the accommodation there was often an Asian char waller who ran what can only be described as a small shop and they would run a tab for you, so if you did not have the money till payday then you could still get your bits and pieces from him but remember payday only gave you a few pounds in the early seventies as the rest was saved for you for when the tour was over you then had enough money for a very good leave.

One night that stands out was a New Year's Eve and we were expecting a very busy night but in fact it was very calm and we got to past midnight with no incidents, now bear in mind that when the lads went on R & R to Germany they would bring back duty free booze as we were only allowed 2 small cans of beer a day and as it was a very quiet night they asked if they could have a drink and I could see no harm in that, so for about an hour or so they all had loads to drink and we then decided it was time to get to bed and I made sure that all of the booze was put away and out of site so I was the last one to go to bed and just as I was about to take my boots off the general alarm sounded, oh shit.

As I was fully dressed I was shouting to the lads to get moving and I grabbed my flak jacket and weapon and ran down to the yard to be told that the guard on the gate had been abducted, as my lads came running down with the infantry soldiers I was telling them what vehicles and who to go where.

Both myself and my drivers were half pissed this could end up in trouble but when everyone was in vehicles, including me, we went off to look for the abducted soldier and in fact found him not to far away where he had been dumped and as the panic was over we could all get back to our base and I stayed in the yard to ensure that all of my section were ok and safely back.

I was a bit worried as I am sure that someone would have noticed that some of the drivers were pissed although nobody noticed that there was one missing. Who was so pissed that the other lads rolled him under the bunk bed and left him there but I was on my way back to the room when it came over the tannoy for me to report to the CO's office and I thought that this was going to be trouble and when the CO said "I want to talk about the response of you and your men" I was cringing he then went on to say how impressed he was that I was one of the first in the yard organising the drivers who were also very quick to get to their vehicles, I did not say it was because they had only just got to bed but at least he thought that the RCT were on the button!!

In the early seventy's there were often small mini protests going on and many of them were young teenagers trying to be seen as grown up and on one occasion when we were out on patrol a large group of teenagers and young men tried to wind us up by singing some republican rebel songs but when I started to sing along with them they all got fed up and walked away, much to the amusement of the rest of the patrol.

R & R was normally taken about half way through a tour but you had to book it early as you could not have all of the drivers away at the same time and of course admin had to book flights or ferry's and if required train tickets for transfers between airports or ferry terminals and your home.

On one occasion I went from Belfast to Liverpool on the ferry then train to London to get there in time for my niece's wedding which for a 4 night R & R brake was pushing it a bit and to help me get around I hired a car but when I took my brother anywhere in the car, he would start laughing every time we stopped at traffic lights and he then explained that he found it very funny that whenever we stopped he said that I was looking at all the surrounding window and doors, just checking as old habits die hard.

It was a good wedding and as both my niece and her fiancé were only16 everyone gave it no chance of lasting and to be fair at the time of writing this book it has only lasted 45 years.

After the wedding it was back to Belfast to carry on with the tour and sometimes I would go out on patrol with the infantry to just get out and about and sometimes if they were a bit short because of other escort duties or sickness then either myself or others would volunteer to help out and on one such occasion we were go down a back alleyway when we heard footsteps and whispering coming from the alley that joined where we were.

We all lifted our weapons and as they came to the corner I shouted for them to stand still only to be totally gobsmacked to hear a voice say "That sounds like Cookey" and lo and behold it was one of my best mates from my school days (DC) who I had heard had joined the army but nothing else and of course we did not have the time nor inclination to stand around chatting with the other lads on both patrols getting rather nervous.

On another occasion I was driving a vehicle for the infantry on a raid of a meeting held in a local public house and the infantry all went in to arrest the participants and myself and other drivers waited outside to guard the vehicles and as they brought out the men from the meeting, I could not believe my eyes as I knew one of the men from one of my previous postings and was sure that he was still serving so I just looked away and did not acknowledge him at all but later in the police station all of the men were put into cells but as we were having a cup of tea some time later he came in with an officer and I then found out that he had been in Belfast for some time and had been working under cover, I am not sure if he carried on after that raid or if he was returned to his unit but that was one hell of a surprise.

In the main the RCT operated 3 types of vehicles in Northern Ireland, the 3 ton truck, a land rover or an armoured pig, now the pig was a real bugger of a vehicle as it was not originally meant to carry that much armour and if you tried to drive a bit quick over a speed bump you would damage the differential.

You would then come to a grinding halt which could be very dangerous in many areas and I am sure that the vehicle rescue lads dreaded hearing of another breakdown in certain areas and another negative with the armoured pig was that it felt like you were inside a tin can and it felt rather agoraphobic, especially if there was more than 4 people in the back and it only needed one of them to fart and life became unbearable.

All of our land rovers had a sort of plastic armour called macrolon (I am not sure about the spelling) which was very good in most circumstances, it was also much lighter than traditional armour and would protect you from low calibre weapons such as a 12 bore shotgun which just bounced off of the side of the land rover although the inside would often have a load of brown smelly stuff that would need cleaning up, yes you are right!!!

Once, in the winter I was told to go as an escort in a 3 ton truck to Aldergrove airport to collect some stuff that had just been flown in but it was the middle of winter and it was freezing cold, now in the roof of the drivers cab was a hole with a canvas cover and this was used for a soldier to stand through the hole with a weapon and in some areas of combat this could have been a machine gun but on this occasion it was just little old me with a rifle, "now the weather outside was frightful" sorry to nick the words of a song but it was bloody cold, so much so that on the return journey I really did not care if there was an ambush as I was so cold I closed the canvas roof and stayed inside the cab to try and survive, which luckily I did.

Our main HQ was a fair way outside of Belfast where we had the main workshops and some recovery teams and all of the admin staff and officers were stationed there and although I only ever went up there on very few occasions it still amazed me as they had a lot more amenities and they were not sleeping 12 to a room like most of the lads down town.

On one occasion we were on patrol with the infantry lads and as often happened a local elderly lady brought out a tray full of mugs and I assume tea but as we went nearer we all noticed that the bloody tea was bubbling and I must say that she even looked surprised and I cannot remember if she dropped the tray or if one of the lads gave it a bash but the so called tea went onto the pavement.

The Falls Road was always one of the most dodgy areas of Belfast and any soldier who served in the area over a twenty year period would tell you the same and if we got a call that one of our pigs (the vehicle and not the military police) had broken down on the Falls Road we went to it as fast as possible before a crowd could form and cause a dodgy situation and of course, to protect the crew of the vehicle.

On one occasion I was asked to drive the CO to a meeting with prominent armed forces personnel and M.P's in Newry but they did not want to draw attention to this meeting so we were given an unmarked civilian registered car for the job and both the CO and myself were to wear civilian clothes.

The problem was that I had no civilian clothes with me so I had to go around and borrow a pair of trousers, a shirt, a jacket and shoes but the only shoes in my size that I could borrow were in fact a pair of trainers and it was either wear them or wear army boots so I chose the trainers, I also had to get a 9mm pistol which was rather difficult to hide in the inside pocket of my borrowed jacket.

We drove down to Newry and arrived after dark, the gates to the house were open and we drove up a very long driveway but as we got closer to the house it was in total darkness and there were no other vehicles parked there and at this point I was wondering if this was a set up and as the CO had his weapon in his hand he felt the same so we parked the car and with our weapons ready we very slowly walked around to the rear of the building where we heard voices and lots of lights were on, wow, I wish I had borrowed some brown trousers.

On entering I saw some people that I recognised but I was then shown upstairs to the nursery where nanny, the children and other drivers and escorts were and at this point nanny asked me to fasten my jacket as the sight of the pistol may scare the children but she said it in such a nice calm way that I immediately did as I was told and she then ensured that we all had food and cups of tea after the children went to bed and the meeting went on for some time and we arrived back in Belfast in the early hours with no further scares or mishaps.

Any tour of Northern Ireland was full of incidents many of which were a bit scary but there was also some funny or nice bits such as on one tour one of the local lady cleaners who bought every soldier a small Christmas present such as a few hankies or a couple of pair of socks,

Nearly all military flights into Belfast went to Aldergrove Airport and most soldiers arrived by a C130 which was an RAF plane used to carry troops, weapons or even small vehicles and we sometimes had to take or pick up stuff from the airport and there were times when some vehicles were ambushed on this route so most vehicles had an infantry escort to ensure everyone safety.

Every tour of Northern has its ups and downs and I have tried to concentrate on the ups but many soldiers got injuries that were only identified many years later but let us hope that they are all now getting the help and support that they need and of course there have been many other conflicts that have happened at the same time or since the troubles ended and those veterans still need the on-going help and support of not only the armed forces but society as a whole.

One of the hardest things I had to do in the army, never mind Northern Ireland was to tell a soldier in my section that his dad had died and this was a soldier who had been in the army for a number of years and had done previous tours but of course, he still found the news very hard to handle but even though we were on active service they still gave him leave to join his family.

At the end of any tour of Northern Ireland you got 2 weeks leave and if you were stationed in Germany you also had a couple of days not at work to get everything sorted such as money ready for your leave but some of the lads spent a lot of time playing cards before going on leave and if you were single you had the choice of going to blighty by plane or if you wanted to drive then you got ferry tickets and during my time in Germany I always drove back to England and on one occasion after Belfast I actually spent a week in a caravan at Pevensey bay in Sussex on my own to de-role and then went and stayed with my brother before returning to Germany.

I had spent nearly 9 years in the army when someone in the squadron office noticed that I had signed on for 9 years and was due to leave the army so I was asked if I wanted to re-sign for the full 22 years and was there any particular posting that I was interested in and after my time with children and young people at the sailing club I asked if I could get a posting to the Army Youth Team which meant you wore civilian clothes, had a civilian flat and car and of course promotion (again) and early in the new year I was told that I had a posting to the Army Youth Team in Bournemouth, wow, what a result,

Early in the New Year I started to have trouble with my eyes and over the years I had a number of incidents involving things hitting me on the head, things like rifles and bricks but I never thought that there would be any problems but others started to notice that my eyes were getting worse.

I was still driving and I told them that I could still see big things like buses, yes, you are right, that went down like a lead balloon and although I was laughing about it when I could not see very well out of one eye my OC decided that I should seek medical advice, now anyone who has been in the forces will tell you that when reporting sick you were often just given 2 codeine and told to report back for work but in my case they were a bit worried and I was admitted to the army hospital in Germany for various tests.

I was then told that I was being transferred to a military hospital in London for further tests and treatment if required and a few days later, together with another couple of soldiers we went on a military aircraft from Germany to Northolt, an RAF base just outside of London and from there we were taken by ambulance to the Royal Herbert Military Hospital near Woolwich.

The hospital was run just like any other army unit, regardless of the fact that you may be very ill or even dying, it made very little difference and people like myself were allowed to wear civilian clothes and we went downstairs to the dining room for all our meals and any other excuse just to get out of the ward as the RSM who was in charge of the ward was a Bastard with a capitol B.

I had only been there a few days when I got the lift to go down and get my lunch but to my utter shock another of the passengers in the lift was H's wife and she told me that she had a job there and that she would tell H that I was in the hospital and she said he would come and visit and sure enough the next day he turned up to visit.

Now H was a West Ham supporter and in those days they recruited people to sell draw tickets and for your reward you got tickets for the home games and it turned out that H was one of those agents and he had tickets for the next evening home game and would I like to go, well I told him that I would love to go but the RSM would never allow it, especially as it was an evening game but H said he would get it sorted.

The next morning I was told by the RSM that he knew I loved football so he had arranged for H to take me to a West Ham game, oh how good of him !! but it was even better for me as H picked me up took me to the game and then dropped me back to the hospital and all of the other lads on the ward were really fed up as they would have loved to have gone to the football if only to get out of the hospital for a couple of hours, H told me that there was another home game in about 10 days and if I would like to go then he would again take me but sadly a few days later I was transferred to the Milbank Military Hospital in the centre of London, next to the Thames for more tests so I had to turn down his offer.

While I was waiting to be transferred to Milbank I had to travel to another hospital in Aldershot to see a specialist as at this point all the clues said that I was going blind and they were desperate to find out why but it was at Aldershot that I first started to worry a bit as the specialist told me it could be very serious as he suspected that there may be a growth and he could not at this stage if it was a benign tumour or cancer that was causing the eyesight to get worse and he was not sure that Milbank could deal with this but they would discuss with me and make the appropriate decision.

To be fair to the Army they did let me have a few days off before my transfer and I went to stay with one of my brothers who then took me to the hospital and you may have noticed that this one was going to be hospital number 3 where it was said that they had better facilities and more expert doctors than the Herbert hospital.

On my arrival to Milbank I and many others were described as "up patients" which meant we got up and got dressed and spent the day either having tests or sat in the day room reading or watching TV which, as I am sure you will appreciate, was as boring as hell but there were 3 things that we soon realised, the first being that our ward was on the ground floor and secondly the window opened and most importantly at night there was a student nurse on duty and she would pull her desk across the entrance to the ward so that we could not get out without her knowledge but as she was a student and a bit weary of us older smarmy gits she never came into the day room.

We very soon realized that so me and another lad found out that there was an off license just round the corner so we would put in a few bob into a kitty and then the two of us would go out of the window and round to the off licence for a crate of beer which we would then take back and when we had finished the beer we would put the empty crate just below the outside of the window before returning it the following night to get another one, now this hospital was not bad, also bear in mind that you could smoke in hospitals and if you were confined to bed they would then give you an ashtray on your side locker otherwise you could walk to the day room to have a fag except during ward rounds.

Another good thing about Milbank was that you could get a 2 or 3 hour pass in the afternoon to get out and about, now I had made good friends with two soldiers.

One of the soldiers had terminal cancer and he was only given a few months to live but he was determined to make the most of it and when I asked him about finding out it was terminal he said that they seemed not to answer his questions directly but sort of hinted that it was terminal (I wonder if they told him not to book a holiday for next year) but he knew it was bad news when they gave him his cigarettes back and told him that he could carry on smoking but he was still there at the hospital for ages.

The other soldier that I made friends with was a young para who had been on exercise to the Far East when he was bitten by some sort of insect and very slowly it started to paralyse him from the neck down and by the time I got to know him he was starting to get feeling back all over his body and he could move his arms enough to steal my toothpaste but as far as I am aware the centre for tropical diseases never did identify the insect that bit him but he was expected to make a full recovery.

As the 3 of us became friends we started to get a pass to go out and even pop into a pub for a beer or two but you had to see us to believe, one was in a wheelchair and needed help to lift his pint (but had no bloody trouble drinking it) one was very short of breath and looked like death warmed up and one had to wear dark glasses until they found out the cause of the failing eyesight, so it was a bit like the blind leading the rest and the local pubs and clubs started to get to know us and one particular strip joint very close to the hospital would let the military in for nothing in the afternoons and they found it very funny every time they saw us 3.

All good things come to an end eventually and the doctors decided that I needed further tests that were not available at that hospital and that they were going to transfer me to a specialist hospital which was the Queens Hospital for Nervous Diseases as it was known at that time but now is just called the Queens Hospital but one of the well-known surgeons there was a man called Roger Bannister who I did get a chance to briefly talk to about athletics but not my medical problems.

In the same ward as me at Queens was an older man who had a problem with what I would call a nervous twitch and as he was talking to you his head would twitch to one side and he was there for some sort of operation to try and help it but this man came from a well-known equestrian family in Sussex and his elderly mother would visit him and sometimes bring him a hamper which included various little treats plus some wine which we all thought was great and for that matter, so did he, for as soon as his mother left he would call us all over to have a look to see what she had brought this time and as he was a really nice (but posh) bloke he would always share what he had and yes, that did include the wine but we had to do it secretly as we were not allowed any alcohol.

There were some really nice other patients and as far as I can remember, as it was over 40 years ago, I was the youngest patient in our ward but I must say that I am sure that we had the best staff in the whole hospital and do remember at this time we were allowed to smoke in the day room and on occasions a nurse would pop in for a quick fag and of course, none of us would say anything to the ward sister or matron.

One of the blokes in our ward came from London and his wife used to come and visit him nearly every day but he was always worried about her getting home after dark and so that she did not have to pay for a telephone call she would phone the day room which had its own phone and let the phone ring 3 times and she would then put the phone down and as nobody answered the phone she did not have to pay.

I thought that it was a lovely way of saving money but at the same time putting his mind at rest.

I had to have a number of horrible tests bearing in mind that they did not have CT or MRI scans available so the only way they could find out any medical information that would help them make a decent diagnosis was to use some techniques that even then were very old.

One of those tests that I think is still used in certain circumstances today is the Lumber Punch which to me sounds like a boxing term but as most of you will know it is a rather large needle put into the base of your spine to extract some fluid that would then help with the diagnosis and I was asked if I wanted to see the needle that was going to be used, now, as you are aware by now I was not the bravest soldier in the army so I declined their offer but when it was over they asked again and I said ok, bloody hell it was about 10 foot long, ok, that may be a little exaggeration but it looked that long to me.

There was one young doctor who kept telling me different things and of course I then thought that it was obvious that I was dying and would not survive the week but after confiding with the other patients and they started to laugh it became clear that this doctor had said the same sort of things to them all, so that at least helped to put my mind at rest.

I was in that hospital for a few months and they carried out every test known to man, and some of those tests left you feeling very ill for a day or two and of course they were the days when people decided to visit including PB's mum and my sister in laws mum which was very nice of them but they both went away thinking I was more seriously ill then I was. But PB visited me on a few occasions while he was on leave as the hospital was not that far from where his mum and dad lived and I must say that ir did cheer me up a lot as when you are in hospital for a long period of time it does get boring and unlike the military hospitals we were not allowed to go out at all and the only place we could go would be down to the shop which was located in the foyer of the hospital.

I had yet another test and every time I think of this test I think that it must have originated from the dark ages but this test was the one that according to the young doctor gave them their diagnosis.

I was taken into what can only be described as a x-ray cell and in the middle of the cell was a very large wheel (I am laughing as I am writing this but I must assure you that this is true) which I was strapped to and they then gave me an injection of dye, they then turned the wheel little by little x-raying at every point, now this seems ok until you are upside down with the blood rushing to your head, yes I have seen this sort of interrogation torture before in many a film and I was very willing to tell them everything I knew but then I remembered it was not interrogation but only a hospital test, thank goodness for the modern scans.

When I told the lads on the ward what happened at the test they thought that I was winding them up and it was only when the ward sister came to see if I was ok that she explained how the test was performed, that they believed me.

Also remember in those days it took some time for the results of any tests to come through and it was a few days before the doctors came to give me the results and when they came to your bedside and pulled the curtains you thought that you may only have days to live!! But they said that they thought that I had a benign tumour that had damaged the nerve going to the optic nerve and this is what was causing the loss of sight in one eye and they could not say if that was it or if it could mean that I went blind totally, now days they would be able to tell you almost exactly what was going on and what the prognosis would be but back then they did not want to commit themselves so it did leave me a bit up in the air, not knowing if I was going to go completely blind or not, although I did quite like the idea of taking my guide dog down to the pub but to this day I am not sure if they were correct or not but as I have only lost most of the sight in one eye and as it has not had a devastating effect on my life apart from being medically discharged from the army which I did not want.

I then had one or two other tests over the next couple of days and also had the good news that the man from the equestrian family had his operation and he was now back to normal and being discharged from hospital and we were all delighted for him.

For me, there was nothing further they could do as they felt that the risks of an operation far outweighed the benefits that may be achieved so after a long time I was finally discharged but only back to Milbank bloody hospital.

I must admit it was a bit like returning home when I got back to Milbank as I was known to the staff and even some of the patients but some had either died or got better or neither of those two scenarios and therefor were just discharged from the forces.

The next step on my journey was to have a meeting with a member of the nursing staff who told me how ill I was and therefor I had to be discharged from the army, now call me fastidious but I did not feel that ill nor was I keen to leave the army but I was also bright enough to realise that there was no way that I could remain in the army.

The next step on this journey was to go before a discharge board where any other options, if there were any, will be discussed and I would then be told that I was being discharged, you see, very straightforward.

The board was made up of a number of (very) old soldiers who were all ex officers and none had a bloody clue as to how I was feeling or to give me any meaningful advice.

It was a bit like being in court with all of the old dodgers sat along a large table and me sat the other side which was very intimidating and even more so when the chair of the panel told me that I was going blind and the first thing I should do was to register as a disabled person and he went on to assure me that this would make it easier for me to get a job, oh how kind, but when I questioned the fact that I did not feel disabled and I felt no worse than a few months earlier when all the tests started they all looked at each other and the chairman then said in a very patronising manner "you must accept that you are disabled" which really got up my nose so it was now time to fight back but in a nice way.

I then asked the chairman if he could jump out of an aircraft and free fall for a few thousand feet, he then informed me with a rather puzzled look on his face that he had never parachuted at all, I then asked if he thought that he could play a full game of football or cross country speed walk for 10k and again he answered no but when I pointed out that I could still do all of those things but I was being advised by the board to apply to become disabled and I just wondered if the board were all registered disabled people and the meeting then came to a rather abrupt end with me being told that I was going to be medically discharged from the army with a lump sum and a monthly pension and I would have a forces resettlement officer who would help and advise me in my transition to civilian life.

I think I saw someone once and he reiterated what the board had said and that I would get a job easier as I did not look disabled and he also told me that all big companies had to employ a percentage of their workforce who were registered disabled, I don't know if that was true.

I was hoping that the whole procedure would take months as life at Milbank was rather cushy and I was happy to stay there for as long as it took but unfortunately it did not take that long and my next move was to go back to Germany to collect belongings and then report to Aldershot for the final discharge.

It all seemed to happen very quickly after that as I suppose the army did not want to pay the wages of a soldier who was no longer going to be a soldier and I returned to my unit in Germany with the news that I had been told that I had a benign tumour and the way everyone looked at me you would have thought that it was terminal and that I would very possibly drop dead very soon, but alas that was not the case and over 40 years later I am still here, at least for the moment.

Although I was not back in Germany for very long it seemed to be one long piss up and what must have been about a thousand goodbyes.

So, off to Aldershot to where that phase in my life started and all the memories remembered in this book but the big question now was where would I live, staying with my brothers for a week on leave is very different from asking if I could live with them so I decided that I would live in Dorking, which I liked and it was where I spent some nice time when on leave with J and he had a great brother whose name I am afraid I cannot recall but he worked for a large insurance firm who at that time had very large offices just on the edge of Dorking and it was him that found me lodgings with an old lady who was very kind to me and another little point was that I fancied their sister who had just left her husband and moved back home.

This book is about my time in the army but I will just mention a couple of things after I left the army which I found rather difficult to come to terms with and one of those was the launderette which I had never used before so when I took my washing to the shop I was looking at the rules, the costs and what the hell to do next when an old lady asked me if I was ok and when I explained she immediately told me how much it would be and then sent me off to the pub (a very wise old lady) and told me to return in an hour and all of my stuff was washed and nicely folded, wow.

Do remember that I had never cooked for myself, apart from the odd curry on the top of an oil stove, my mother cooked for us and then I joined the army and they cooked for me, so this was the first time I had to go shopping.

I had to find out how many small lamb chops there are to the pound in weight and then casually ask the landlady of the local pub how she does her chops!!! I would do a rather large saucepan of mince and potatoes and this would last days and after a few days it became a mince and potato curry.

I was totally out of my depth, I did not know many people, I had no idea what I wanted to do for a career and it seemed like getting a job was going to be hard.

I do remember taking my mates sister out for a meal to a restaurant in Dorking and when we arrived there was a very well-known actor and film star who lived just outside of Dorking dining with a group of friends and very soon after we arrived the actor got up onto the table and dropped his trousers and underpants, well, it nearly put me off my starter but I suppose that was the age we lived in because nowadays other customers would walk out and the police called but in this case the manager just said "very good sir now will you please get dressed" which he did without question and we all got on with our meal.

To be honest I had been told by everyone at the hospital and at Aldershot that getting a job would be easy as everyone would like to employ an ex-soldier and to a degree that was correct and to be honest every job that I applied for I got an interview and every time I thought that it was going well they would then ask me why I had left the army.

When I told them that I was medically discharged their attitude dramatically changed, this happened a few times and when I told the landlord of the local pub he said, why tell them, just say that 10 years was enough and you want a new career in Civvie street, so that is what I did and got the next job that I applied for which I did not end up taking as it was for a master of arms (security) on a cruise ship that did the UK to Australia run and it had not long left so I would have to wait until it returned which would have been about another 10 weeks and I needed a job sooner so I started as a private detective, now that may sound rather exciting but the truth was it was rather boring for most of the time but it did give me money and I kept looking for another job, but just like a London bus, you wait for ages then two come along together, one was a job as a children's sailing instructor in Poole in Dorset.

My old OC came to visit me to see how I was and if I had started on a new career and when he found that I was a bit fed up he said that he had a job offer for me as the Corps sports officer, this was a well-paid job with the opportunity to travel all over the world with the various sports teams but I was out of the army and did not see myself as one of those sad people who still had to rely on the forces, so I turned down that offer and went to Dorset at the end of March 1976 to help start up and work at the sailing school and that was a pretty good decision as it was one of the hottest summers on record.

My mate PB came out of the army about the same time and I think his mum and dad had settled near to Tonbridge in Kent so that is where PB settled and as I said earlier in this book he was a very good footballer and he started playing for Tonbridge as a semi-professional footballer and on one occasion I went to watch him play and I was surprised to see that his manager was a 1966 world cup winner which PB loved.

Words and Sayings

Forces remembered

Most of the words or sayings that I have used in this book will be well known to any forces veterans

Weasel piss, this is used to describe very weak beer or other   alcohol.

Pillock, someone acting in a rather stupid way.

PTSD, I am sure that you all now know about this condition called Post Traumatic Stress Disorder which is not funny and is suffered by many ex service personnel who battle for some time to get back where they were.

Fags, no, not the American translation but it is what we often call cigarettes.

Blighty, what many servicemen over many years have called England or the UK.

Pissed, Drunk

Shit Faced, very, very drunk.

GHM, a Going Home Machine, which if you saw a plane when serving abroad you would often refer to it as a GHM.

Compo Ration, just tins of food that had no sell by date on them and in the main they were bloody horrible but I must say that the apricot pudding was fantastic.

Thunder box, a hole in the ground covered by a big box with a hole in the top so that you could have a comfortable shit and anyone in command would call it a field toilet.

A Technicolor Yawn, Most people would call it vomiting but a yawn was more acceptable to say in case people were eating.

Stevedore or what was known in Civvie Street as a Docker or one who worked in the dockyards.

Tango Sierra, radio talk for tough shit

Foxtrot Oscar, radio talk for f*** off

C.O. Commanding officer of a regiment

O.C. Officer commanding of a squadron within a regiment

R.S.M. Regimental sergeant major, the most senior of the non-commissioned ranks in the regiment.

S.S.M. Squadron sergeant major, the most senior of the non-commissioned ranks in the squadron.

The Clap, this was not audience participation or appreciation but a sexually transmitted disease.

Bulled Boots, highly polished but not with a brush but with a cloth and this is where the saying spit and polish came from

Boxed Blankets, this was a way of folding your blankets so that they then looked like a box.

Pace Stick, used by the RSM to measure the length of the pace.

Bullshit, there are couple of explanations but the most common one used means it is a lie or miss-information.

MRS, a medical receiving station which was like a small hospital for minor injuries or illness.

Great People and Songs

Friends & Songs remembered

The following people were some of my greatest mates during my times in the army and if any of you are reading this book and recognise yourself then please feel free to contact me on Facebook and the reason I have not used their full names is out of respect as some of them may no longer be with us or they have not told their wives or partners that they had friends like me who were a pain in the arse.

John J, he was from Kent where I now live and he was one of my first friends in basic training.

Tich A, we were great friends and I spent a lot of time in Salford and he also stayed with us in both London and Kent

John G, who lived just down the road from Tich, he was in the army as well and we got on well and I even went to visit him and his wife when I was stationed in Kent.

Ragger or Rags, I am not sure if he was a London or an Essex boy but he was a great laugh and I cannot be certain but it may have been him that married the young Geordie girl in Newcastle.

Noddy K, he was a smashing Scotsman with a great sense of humour and we were good friends.

H was from Hull and he had a German father and it was him that taught us the phrase genug es genug, (I think I have said it correctly) which means enough is enough in German and he also taught me the songs mentioned earlier about Hull.

Mick P, I believe that he was from the midlands and prior to joining the army he played non-league football for Burton Albion and at the present time they are a club in the football league.

Scouse H, who was one of my best friends in the army and I was best man at his wedding but although he sounded like a scouse, he was in fact from Birkenhead.

Cold Arse, He should require no introduction as he is mentioned a few times.

Big Jock M, otherwise known as Tiny as he was very tall and came from Thurso in

Northern Scotland and he was a very nice gentle sort of bloke.

Geordie D, Fred, from Newcastle with his black rimmed glasses it was his parents' house that we stayed in for the wedding and his mother that washed and returned my underpants,

Taffy Jones, I was with him in Singapore and I have used his full name so the millions of Welshmen can say it was them and even by using his name he cannot be identified.

Nobby Clarke, anyone who was called Clarke was always known as Nobby, now don't ask me why but as above he could not be identified by his name but I did serve with him in Bielefeld and if I remember correctly we were together in Catterick and got posted together to Germany.

Andy A, I met in trade training, got posted together to Catterick and then met up again in Singapore.

There were so many parts of army life that I loved, yes there were some parts that were not so good but overall the good far outweighed the not so good and one of the good things was no matter where in the UK you were from; there was probably a song about the place.

Many of the songs that we sang could be called rugby songs and I am sure that they are still being sung in both the army and at hundreds of rugby clubs up and down the country.

All of the Yorkshire men sang "on Ilkley Moor Bar Tat" which to this day I still remember a lot of the words.

I belong to Glasgow and the Northern Lights of old Aberdeen I still sing to this day.

If you came from Lancashire all of those lads called it the cheese song as it sounded like "cheese a lassie from Lancashire" I did think it was funny the first time I heard it.

I was always in the minority but always sang "maybe it's because I'm a Londoner" and of course over the years many lads from all over the UK got to know the words

One of the lads from Hull taught us a couple of songs and remember that there was no Humber Bridge and the song was Called "Will they ever Bridge the Humber" or will we have to keep on going round by Goole another part of that song that I still remember is the following-:

In 1966 Harold Wilson was in a fix

With his overall majority down to two, so Barbara Castle came to see what she could do,

She told them on that day, they would get their Humber Bridge

And there won't be much delay, but still we're waiting for our Humber Bridge (1974)

Now that may not be word perfect but you get the idea that some things stay with you forever including another Hull song about the fact they wanted to build a public toilet underneath a statue of Queen Victoria and part of the words of the song were-: "she's not amused she's been abused they have sat her on a toilet"

I could of course go on forever with songs like "I belong to Glasgow" or if you are a Geordie then how about "The Blaydon Races"

Of course, every regiment had their own songs and ditties and the RCT were no exception, our song was a little long winded with various versions depending on where you were stationed but one of the verses that I remembered was the following.

Here comes the sergeant major
Driving up the front
Some say he's a senior rank
But some say he's a **** please insert your own word.

Plus of course the many other dirty songs that I will not write down all the words here but they would make a great book, songs such as -:
Two sweaty socks and an old French letter

Put your sweet lips a little closer to my knob.

Mary of the mountain glen.

The Last Post

The end of an era

We now come to the end of this part of my life and this my second book which I hope that people will enjoy but I have the feeling that if you are a forces veteran then you will enjoy this book more than someone who has not served and many of the stories and the names of colleagues will bring back many memories that will either make you smile or cringe.

I was lucky enough to meet some smashing people, both soldiers and civilians and to have travelled to many parts of the world which gave me the appetite for travel which has never left me and at the time of writing this book I have been to over 50 countries, some more than once and still counting and saving my pennies for further overseas adventures.

I still use many sayings that I picked up in the army and some of my friends who also served will often smile and say they have not heard that saying since their army service.

May I say a very sincere thank you to everyone who has bought and read this book, as I write this I have a great feeling that this book will do very well and who knows, it could even be made into a film one day,

Manufactured by Amazon.ca
Bolton, ON

14901912R00197